Church and Diakonia
in the Age of COVID-19

Reimagining Church as Event: Perspectives from the Margins
Series Editors: George Zachariah and Sudipta Singh

In these eleven volumes, a collective of Indian theologians envisions Church as an Event that happens in particular contexts in the life of the communities at the margins. They argue that in the life of the communities who experience on their bodies the violence and hegemony of dominant power relations, morality, and religious dogmas and practices, the church happens as countercultural experiences that disrupt the logic of the prevailing order. These experiences enable and empower them to affirm and celebrate their differences, knowledges and beauty even as they weave their liberation. Church as event is a call to rising to life, creating life-flourishing communities that live out the foretaste of the reign of God.

Titles in this Series

Church and Religious Diversity Joshua Samuel and Samuel Mall
Church and Gender Justice Aruna Gnanadason
Faith in the Age of Empire Y.T. Vinayaraj
Dalitekklesia: A Church from Below Raj Bharat Patta
Church and Climate Justice Vinod Wesley
Church and Disability Samuel George
Church and Diakonia in the Age of COVID-19 Mothy Varkey
Decolonising Oikoumene Gladson Jathanna
Church and Human Sexuality Arvind Theodore
With Many Voices: Liturgies in Context Viji Varghese Eapen (Ed.)
The Word becoming Flesh George Zachariah

Church and Diakonia
in the Age of COVID-19

Mothy Varkey

2020

Church and Diakonia in the Age of COVID-19- jointly published by the Indian Society for Promoting Christian Knowledge (ISPCK), Post Box 1585, Kashmere Gate, Delhi-110006 and Council for World Mission, Singapore-338729.

ISBN: 978-93-88945-83-7

Kindle Edition: 978-93-88945-96-7

Cover Illustration Credit : Immanuel Paul Vivekanandh K

Laser typeset by

ISPCK, Post Box 1585, 1654, Madarsa Road, Kashmere Gate, Delhi-110006 • *Tel:* 23866323

e-mail: ashish@ispck.org.in • ella@ispck.org.in
website: www.ispck.org.in

Dedication

*This book is dedicated to **Smt. K. K. Shailaja Teacher**, the indefatigable "coronavirus slayer", health minister of Kerala, India. Under her committed and instinctive leadership, built with intelligence and empathy on a foundation of unflinching honesty, all the public servants and healthcare professionals in the state worked on the frontlines of the COVID-19 pandemic. Shailaja teacher transformed the healthcare system in Kerala into a democratic movement and a people's initiative in the pursuit of handling the pandemic.*

Contents

Foreword

DISCERNMENT AND RADICAL ENGAGEMENT (DARE) is an initiative of the Council for World Mission (CWM) to enable faith communities to *clarify what it means to engage in* public witness to God's justice and peace in a corrupt and conflicted world.

> The mission of DARE is conceived as the coming together of (a) the *radical soul* of discernment and sense-making in theology and biblical criticism; (b) the yearnings for *signifying engagement* that rise out of the slums of modernism and the valleys of despair; and (c) the commitment to redemption songs that *inspire disturbance* at the hubs of power.

As part of the DARE initiative, each region of CWM is invited to prepare and share biblical and theological resources on current themes and issues being considered by CWM, drawing upon the experiences and resources from the region.

Interfaith Engagement, Ecumenism and Inclusive communities against dehumanising social categorisations are the themes for the book series undertaken by the South Asia region of CWM. The thrust is centred on **Reimagining Church as Event: Perspectives from the Margins**. It calls to the fore persons living in the margins and highlights their voice, their narratives and their passion for a rearrangement of life in communities, as we know it, and a commitment to rise to life and to break out from Babylon. These books are intended for the use of lay people, pastors and evangelists as well as for theological students and seminaries. The series offer stories and narratives, analyses, liturgical resources, biblical, theological and ethical reflections, and missional/praxis proposals.

Church is an event that happens at the margins of contemporary life. Church happens as an epiphanic event where the divine presence is manifested and experienced in the pathos, struggles, contestations and harmonies of everyday existence. Church happens in those spaces where we celebrate the presence of Jesus, the Christ, in the flourishing of life. Church happens when we are transformed by one another, and inspired and enabled to engage in the transformative politics of the reign of God. Church happens whenever and wherever spirit-filled communities reclaim their subversive moral agency and contest the logic and practices of domination and exclusion. Church happens when the community experiences the healing power of the wounded healer and join Jesus in this risk-taking mission, despite the wounds we bear. To reimagine Church requires courage and commitment to engage in the mission of nurturing and organising communities of resistance and healing. This book series is a humble attempt at exposing and encouraging this radical expression of Church.

I appreciate and thank all those who are associated with this series, the authors, the contributors, the publishers and the editors. I commend this book series in the hope and prayers that they will help the faith communities in South Asia, and beyond, to *discern God's presence in community and dare to engage* in ways that re-present the God of life in communities and in the public square, *Rising to Life: Living out the New Heaven and New Earth.*

Colin Cowan
General Secretary
Council for World Mission

Introduction

*Vincent Rajkumar**

For over a decade, we have been living through consecutive global crises that have brought the concept of governance in national and global politics to the forefront. Like the other crises of the past decade, COVID-19 is also a test of governance, where competence, transparency, trust, capacity, effective leadership and efficiency lie at the core of success in fighting the pandemic. The extent to which states possess the capacity to address the crisis, the degree of inclusiveness through governance, and the complementary relationship between inclusive governance and democracy are prime issues that we need to focus on in assessing our response to the epidemic. Over the past three months, the phrase "the new normal" has been used quite a bit in reference to the COVID-19 pandemic. The new normal is not just referring to life after the pandemic, for we have no idea when that day will come. As we grope our way in the dark to find out what the new normal is going to be, we may well discover that a good part of the world is going to be different and that COVID-19 is the harbinger of change taking control of all our lives.

The current situation remains uncertain at all levels: public health, social, economic and international. We are now facing a new, hard and long road to a "normality" in many parts of the world. Yet this "normality" would not have the same definition as before the crisis. The COVID-19 pandemic is just the tip of the iceberg of converging global crises—biodiversity loss, droughts, mega-fires, floods, rising temperatures, pollution, ocean acidification—in a world where we value economy over ecology, where greed supplants care, where "rights" screen us to responsibilities, where we worship a golden idol over Mother Earth. The unbridled plunder of nature in the name of economic growth at any cost—from deforestation, habitat degradation and fragmentation, climate change, to species extinction— pushes more and more people into direct contact and conflict with animals that carry dangerous pathogens. In this context, the prevailing opinion that culture and nature are somehow separate must become obsolete. Such a deceptive view of culture- nature disconnect is at the root of our utilitarian view of the world based on infinite economic growth; only by recognising their intrinsic value and interdependence can we hope to pave the way forward towards living in harmony with nature and people. To manage the ongoing crisis and to better anticipate the next one, we need to introduce an interdisciplinary "One Health" approach in a concerted manner in order to foster the health of ecosystems and of plants, animals and humans living within them, to increase their resilience and to thereby reduce the risk of new pandemics.

A time like this raises significant theological concerns, many of which the church needs to explore as it reflects in the days to come. The issues raised by the coronavirus pandemic do not concern merely the life of the church, its worship, and ways in which pastoral care is extended to those in need. There are profound questions about society, and the nature of the human community, to which the church needs to respond theologically. The diaconal church which involves in the service of people is expected to respond both reactively and proactively: reactively by intervening to support the most vulnerable people in our communities, who are impacted by COVID-19; proactively by advocating for and with marginalised and vulnerable people and looking to the longer-term consequences of the pandemic. It is in rediscovering the riches of our Christian heritage that we will be able to reflect more deeply on who we are as a church and to examine critically the manifestations of ecclesial life which we have hitherto taken for granted and the ways in which we have sought to sustain our common life under lockdown. It is only on the basis of a renewed theology that we will be able to address coherently the ethical questions that confront us in the present and the future.

The author in this volume narrates in detail the pandemic crisis on the livelihood of the poor, and the public health emergency which emerged as a humanitarian crisis. The author not only deals with the virus that caused the pandemic illness but also economic and environmental viruses. In sorting out these crisis he establishes *the interconnection between the human world and the world of nature and the need for its independence and interconnectedness to avoid any such pandemics in future*. In his narration, he exposes the failures of the political governance in this regard and at the same time reveals the hierarchical church structures that refuse to see this interconnection. He reaffirms that the mode of Christian witness of our early church was not preaching but permeation. While recognising the service rendered by the church in the past, the author emphasises the need to reconnect with its faith articulation as he finds it relevant for the church to build up the interconnection between culture and nature through its life and service. According to him, *ekklēsia* and diakonia. are integrally related. The Christian mission to society becomes true diakonia only when the social and transformative work of the church is directed towards a wider mission paradigm in the transformation of the socio-economic structures. Here church becomes an event. As the church seeks to relate its mission to the world outside in diakonia, it should also be prepared to undergo a process of self-criticism where structures and identities irrelevant to the mission are repeatedly challenged with the central message of the crucified Jesus. In this process of mission to the world and the openness to meaningfully transform one's own structures, the author hopes that the church would constantly redefine its borders and margins as it strives to become a restorative and transforming presence in the world.

*The Rev. Dr. Vincent Rajkumar** is the director of the Christian Institute for the Study of Religion and Society.

Acknowledgements

First and foremost, I thank God, the source of my being and in whom I exist, whose amazing grace has guided and moulded me all my life, especially throughout the writing of this CWM book project. My sincere thanks to Sudpita Singh, Council for World Mission, for including me too as one of the contributors in the book series "Reimagining Church as Event: Perspectives from the Margins." I am deeply grateful to him for his capable supervision, incisive comments, wholehearted affection and unreserved trust and encouragement throughout the course of this book project. I am also grateful to George Zachariah. I could not have wished for a more unassuming mentor in this journey, as he patiently corrected my oversights and fallacious reasoning. He was decisively influential towards the crafting of my arguments with brotherly care and academic precision. It is my joy and honour to express my deep gratitude to Rev. Dr. Vincent Rajkumar and Dr. Revelation E. Velunta for their meaningful and comprehensive introduction and afterword. I would like to express my sincere appreciation to Immanuel Paul Vivekanandh for the intense and brilliant cover design. Special thanks to Sam Abraham for his careful editing and invaluable comments. I express my heartfelt gratitude to ISPCK for publishing this volume.

Prologue

The virus is mankind's ultimate predator.

Robin Cook, *Virus*

From now on it can be said that plague was the concern of all of us.

Albert Camus, *The Plague*

COVID-19 is a once-in-a-century health crisis. But it also gives us a once-in-a-century opportunity to shape the world our children will inherit—the word we want.

Dr. Tedros Adhanom Ghebreyesus

At the end of Albert Camus' novel *The Plague* (1947), its central character Dr. Bernard Rieux, who is in charge of treating the afflicted, realises that as the plague recedes the survivors would honour their dead and return to normal life as if nothing happened even though the virus could make a comeback anytime. To those of us who are consumed by the thoughts of COVID-19, the novel provides enough resources to understand the pandemic as an event in time and space rather than as a singular challenge. This is significant in the wake of a potential viral genocide for the first time, after the use of atom bombs during World War II; in terms of the leading causes of death worldwide we are aware of the ravages of malaria, tuberculosis, AIDS, Ebola and more, not to speak of the high maternal and infant mortality rates in many parts of the world.

According to the economic historian Niall Ferguson,

> There have been two pandemics in history that killed nearly a third of humanity. One in the time of the ancient Romans, the Antonine Plague, and of course the Black Death of the mid-14th century. There was no way of knowing in January if this was the big one. The 1918-19 influenza killed 3% of the world's population—not in the same league as the Black Death, but 3% of today's world population is a pretty big number. So getting people to realize the risk in January, when we knew almost nothing except that there was an infectious disease, that it was going from human to human, and that it was killing people, was difficult.[1]

The World Health Organization (WHO), on 11 March 2020, declared COVID-19 (an acronym for Coronavirus Disease 2019) a pandemic, which meant that the virus was spreading rapidly in almost all nations of the world.[2] The number of COVID cases worldwide at that time was just over 100,000. It was later estimated that the death toll of the immunocompromised would swell to hundreds of thousands.

The crisis of a lifetime, like COVID, could possibly push the world towards a 'Seneca cliff'[3] owing to the already fragile and overloaded economic systems, resource depletion and climate change. As political activist, author and philosopher Cornel West says, "This crisis is just revealing the problems in our world, that have been simmering under the surface for years."[4] For activist and writer Arundhati Roy, "It is the wreckage of a train that has been careening down the track for years."[5] Put differently by Ugo Bardi, professor in Physical Chemistry at the University of Florence, "The coronavirus is not a cause, it is a trigger."[6]

COVID-19 exposes an unparalleled global vulnerability, mainly for two reasons. First, as the Italian philosopher Giorgio Agamben argues, the pandemic has led to the "erasure of fellow human beings."[7] As a result, human community has become a cluster of potential carriers of coronavirus, "an invisible enemy that can nestle in any other human being." Since the "'enemy isn't somewhere outside, it's inside us,' our common humanity intrinsically constitutes a security threat."[8] The fact that threat to humanity is no longer from outside, but from inside, reverses the very logic of security. Second, in the view of Judith Butler, American philosopher and gender theorist, the level of risk in contracting the virus is very high for human beings because they share a common biological space/surface: "We are impressed upon by the environment, social worlds and intimate contact. That impressionability and porosity define our embodied social lives."[9] It shows the interconnected and interdependent character of bodily and social existence. These reciprocal and material modes of shared existence explain the height of human vulnerability to viral infection.

In the Indian context, if we examine the higgledy-piggledy situation after the pronouncement of the nationwide lockdown as a preventive measure against COVID, it becomes clear that it is not just the shared historical and biological existence that exposed the poor and the migrant labourers to danger, but the intersection of politics, caste, class, gender, religion, and the pandemic. India reported the first confirmed case of coronavirus infection on 30 January 2020 in the state of Kerala. But the national government was occupied with other major political events in February: the historic visit of United States President Donald Trump ("Namaste Trump"), the Delhi state Assembly elections and the communal riots in North East Delhi that rendered hundreds homeless. And when the WHO announced COVID-19 a global pandemic, the vital piece of news was lost in the coverage of the collapse of the Congress government in Madhya Pradesh and the drama thereafter.

Finally, on 24 March 2020 at 8 p.m., Prime Minister Narendra Modi announced a lockdown for the 1.35 billion people in the country, giving Indians less than four hours notice before the order took effect, and asked them to endure the disruption of their lives with stoicism. Life was brought to a standstill. Thousands of migrant labourers, almost none wearing masks, marched close together to far-off villages, potentially spreading the virus deep into the countryside. Revisiting the French existentialist philosopher Simone de Beauvoir's memorable line from *The Second Sex*—"One must not think that simple juxtaposition of the right to vote and a job amounts to total liberation; work today is not freedom"—in these times of the pandemic seemed relevant in the context of India.

According to a United Nations report, "The coronavirus can infect and kill the young, as well as the old, the rich, the poor, or those with underlying health conditions. It does not respect race, colour, sex, language, religion, sexual orientation or gender identity, political or other opinion, national, ethnic or social origin, property, disability, birth or any other status. The virus does not discriminate."[10] In theory, all of us are vulnerable to the infection. But this seemingly unbiased statement of "we are all in this together" from the UN was awfully redundant and blatantly apathetic as was seen in many countries.

As UN Secretary General Antonio Guterres rightly said, "While the virus does not discriminate, its impacts do."[11] American writer and activist Rebecca Solnit's view is perhaps more informing and poignant: "Coronavirus does discriminate, because that's what humans do."[12]Nearly everyone in the world is, or will be, affected by this pandemic, but each of us is affected differently. Some of us are financially devastated, some are gravely or fatally ill while many have already died, and some face discrimination outside the home or violence within it. The pandemic is a spotlight that illuminates underlying problems—economic inequality, racism, casteism, patriarchy. As Guterres warns us, the coronavirus outbreak could turn into a human rights crisis as it could give some countries an excuse to adopt repressive measures for reasons unrelated to the pandemic.

Unlike in other parts of the world, India is not new to the practice of social and physical distancing. It has been historically and inherently deep-rooted in the form of caste; it has been used as a socially-sanctioned system to collectively regulate and discriminate against lower castes and Dalits in India. The state's reaction to the virus in India has been premised on characteristic biases such as the caste-class hierarchy and its conterminous affiliations. Arguing that the coronavirus affected Bollywood actor Amitabh Bachchan and his family living in one of the most luxurious bungalows in Mumbai and the *Chamar* and *Musahar* communities living in the squalid ghettos on Mumbai's periphery equally is an effort to homogenise and normalise the population while 'invisiblising' those who are at the bottom of the socio-economic hierarchy of the caste system.

Regardless of the aetiology of the virus, its transmission and propagation has evidently been caste-class based. The *Yadani* community (a community engaged in clearing waste and cleaning drains) of Andhra Pradesh was barred from purchasing essentials such as food and medicine by upper caste people, and the children of the *Musahar* community in Varanasi survived by eating grass. Notwithstanding its noble intent, the lockdown served as a lockdown from access to food, water, shelter, medicines, livelihood and employment for many whose lives were just not important enough for the government's consideration. Millions of Dalits migrated to various urban cities to escape caste discrimination, social oppression and economic deprivation. But COVID-19 has brought back all what they were hoping to get away from into their lifeworld.

The caste system is that butterfly whose flapping wings have an effect on all kinds of interactions of an individual. From the way one dresses and lives to the way in which one earns a living and makes a livelihood, caste is a compelling factor that dictates everything, including the effect of this virus. It is caste-based jobs such as scavenging, sanitation, drain-cleaning and its minimal social value and inadequate remunerations that make Dalit and Adivasi communities more susceptible to the fatal risks of COVID-19. Therefore, "the popular belief that COVID-19 is much more unbiased than most of us is itself smothered with biases which stems from the subsisting caste-class privilege."[13]

The pandemic also works like a political lifeline for authoritarian bigots, racists and fascist regimes. It has brought to the fore endemic injustices and discriminations that have always existed in our healthcare, economy and government. Whatever it is, coronavirus has forced the systems of life to a juddering halt like nothing else could. It has taunted digital surveillance, biometric controls at immigration checkpoints and every kind of security measures set up to curb terrorism. There is no room for patients at hospitals so much so that the sick are dumped in corridors. There is an uptick in panic in many countries. Household staples, hand sanitisers and other hygiene essentials have consistently been out of stock during the outbreak, whether at big-box stores, at bodegas or on Amazon. Despite the authorities stressing there was no shortage, people in places like Sydney were stockpiling even toilet paper.[14] The vanishing of toilet paper from store shelves is just an addendum or footnote in a panicky account of the crisis.

There is a lot of talk about returning to 'normal' after the COVID-19 outbreak. People are anxiously trying to make the future more financially and politically steady either by replicating the past or by sewing the future to their past and refusing to accept the pandemic pandemonium in the present. But the rupture is immediate, epic and factual. There will be no return to what we hitherto envisaged as 'normal'; normal never was. 'Normal' has not worked for a vast majority of the world's population. "Normal was a crisis," says climate activist Greta Thunberg.[15]

Sonya Renee Taylor, the founder of 'The Body is Not an Apology' movement, argues it succinctly: "Our pre-corona existence was not normal other than we normalised greed, inequity, exhaustion, depletion, extraction, disconnection and confusion."[16] Therefore, nothing could be more enslaving and unscrupulous than a return to 'normality.'[17] At this crucial juncture, such a "wasting disease of normalcy" is absolutely a deathtrap.[18] The Slovenian philosopher and cultural theorist Slavoj Žižek in his new book, *Pandemic!: Covid-19 Shakes the World*, persuasively contends that the "new normal will have to be constructed on the ruins of our old lives, or we will find ourselves in a new barbarism whose signs are already clearly discernible."[19] There is no post-COVID. Niall Ferguson puts it poignantly, "This virus is to social life what HIV was to sexual life."[20]

According to the political theologian Joerg Rieger, the logic of COVID-19 and the potential socio-economic nosedive is that "situations of crisis can help us develop a clearer sense of what the world really looks like, for better or worse."[21] There have been diverse and often disappointing responses to the crisis of COVID-19, which in fact is an opportunity to reconfigure the world we live in and the global forces that are shaping it. Panicking is certainly not the way to combat any pandemic, which in reality would trivialise the intensity of the crisis. As Žižek opines, "The strange counterpart of this kind of excessive fear is the absence of panic when it would have been fully justified."[22] This is not a good approach.

Equally abortive is the myopic theory of American and Eurocentric intellectuals who attempt to naturalise the crisis as a cyclic process.[23] This is already outlined by the likes of William Strauss and Neil Howe in their book *The Fourth Turning: An American Prophecy: What the Cycles of History Tell Us About America's Next Rendezvous with Destiny*. Strauss and Howe base their argument on a provocative 'generational theory.' By looking at five hundred years of American history, the authors uncover a distinct theorised pattern that history moves in cycles of historical generational persona (archetypes), and each cyclical saeculum (usually spanning 80 to 90 years) will last about the length of a long human life, each composed of four eras or 'turnings.' After each cycle, a crisis recurs in America and is followed by a recovery. Such an appalling narrative intentionally brought up during this contagion normalises and regularises capitalism's fiascos and its rendezvous with destiny.

Another self-defeating diversion is the conspiracy theory that COVID-19 is not a pandemic but a 'Plandemic.'[24] The now mainstream conspiracy theory comes in two varieties (often combined with partisan politics and pseudoscience): those who doubt the virus' severity (endorsed by President Donald

Trump) and those who suggest it might be a bioweapon. It is important to know how and where the virus originated and how it spread and whether there was any unconscionable negligence or delay on the part of China in alerting the rest of the world with regard to its spread. Trump and other vociferous sections of the US who are immune to evidence have already, without a global inquiry, declared China criminally responsible.[25] But the corollary is that conspiracy theorists thrive during a pandemic if the political culture and public space are dysfunctional. According to Amy Davidson Sorkin, the American author and journalist, this vacuum fittingly explains the perfect matrix of a "conspiratorialist feedback loop." She says: "The less you trust, the more you search for alternative authorities, and the more susceptible you are to untrustworthy figures who maintain their position by attacking what is true."[26]

Taking cue from the Italian Marxist philosopher and historian Antonio Gramsci, the Christian community has to reclaim itself in this interregnum poised between the so-called 'normal' and the 'new normal.' Because of its long history crossing geographical terrains and territories, the Christian community's faith rejoinder to the morbid symptoms of crisis situations are often inconsistent—and the continuing pandemic is no exception. Some Christian leaders like Billy Prewitt, Ralph Drollinger, Robert Jeffress and John Piper have offered bizarre and insensitive self-righteous judgements that COVID-19 pandemic chaos is God's punishment on sinful cities and arrogant nations akin to the plagues in the book of Exodus. Some gullible Christian leaders spread the conspiracy theories.

As a way to bring spiritual healing to people, innovative religious leaders like Father Scott Holmer in Maryland, Father Père de Lestapis in France and Father Brian Mahoney in Boston started offering a "drive-through confession" in the parking lot of the church. One church in Louisiana defied public-health guidelines because they believed in the rash providentialism that their faith provides immunity from the virus and encouraged people to welcome "potential martyrdom." Biblical scholars such as Elizabeth Castelli and Candida Moss argue that such acts of defiance echo the witness of the early church. Many churches in the US filed lawsuits against government orders to close churches. As the New Testament scholar N.T. Wright rightly observed, these are only "knee-jerk would-be Christian reactions" of those who believe that the Bible has explanations for all phenomenon.[27] Our concern should be, in the words of William Lamar IV, the pastor of Metropolitan African Methodist Episcopal Church in Washington, "how bad theology is killing us."[28] However, Bishop Raymond Centène of Vannes in Brittany, in northwest France, has ripped providentialists who seek communion at all costs in the midst of a pandemic by saying they are "tempting God" through their reckless behaviour:

> Obedience to civil laws that is not a concession made out of weakness; it is a Christian's duty…. It is necessary to distinguish between conscientious objection that could compromise God's plan…[and obeying] laws aimed at safeguarding public health… the heroic example of saints who distinguished themselves for their fearless[ness] in plagues of the past was their own decision to put themselves at risk, and not others.[29]

Firing a salvo in his uphill run for the next presidential election, Trump hastily declared houses of worship as 'essential services' and asked the Governors to reopen them: "We want our churches and our places of faith and worship, we want them to open…. In America, we need more prayers, not less." As of August 2020, coronavirus had killed over 150,000 Americans. It might be essential to his political future as his electoral base has been eroding. But the issue here is the notion of 'opening' and 'reopening' the church and the meaning of worship as 'essential service.'

This does elicit theological interrogations, imaginations and intercessions. Is the church a mere physical building to 'close' and 'open'? Are opening the church and conducting prayers the ultimate expression of the diakonia of the church? How does this opening and closing of the church sit with the historical life and crucifixion of Jesus and the diakonia to which he had called the community of the faithful into being? Can the church and worship be insensitive to people's historical life struggles? What does the church exist for then? If worship is essential, then what does the diakonia of the church mean? Is diakonia essential? How does 'going' to the church differ from 'being' the church? As the American Protestant minister and political activist William Barber II convincingly writes, "Houses of worship are not essential, but true worship is"; it means listening to the voice of COVID-19 victims because all human struggles are faith issues/concerns.[30] This explains why the Council for World Mission (CWM) is taking the lead to reimagine 'ἐκκλησία' and 'διακονία' in the context of plagues, pandemics and pestilences.

Our proposed task to reinvent/reclaim ἐκκλησία and διακονία in the context of COVID-19 must begin with reclaiming their exact semantic, theological and political nuances. First, decolonise the word ekklēsia. The Greek word ἐκκλησία (ekklēsia) means assembly or gathering. But the early translators of the King James Bible (KJB) translated the word ekklēsia as 'church.'[31] Consequently, ekklēsia became a hierarchical authority, outside the local assembly, that rules over the local congregation. King James authorised the organised royal religion of the empire—the Church of England—to translate the Bible in 1611. His mandate to follow the 'Bishops' Bible' for translation and to keep the old ecclesiastical words affected the translation of the Greek word ekklēsia.[32] By making Bible translation a royal/imperial project, King James turned ekklēsia into an extension of his jurisdiction. By decolonising the translation process of the word ekklēsia as in the KJB, we make ekklēsia a people's assembly.

It is also argued that in the earlier Greek, 'church' was pronounced 'ku-ri-a-kos' or 'ku-ri-a-kon,' which means pertaining to the 'kurios' ('lord'). The Greek 'kuriakos' eventually came to be used in the Old English form as 'cirice' ('kee-ree-ke'), then 'churche' ('kerke'), and eventually 'church' in its traditional pronunciation. That is, the translators were not translating the Greek word 'kuriakos,' as one might expect. Rather, they were substituting an entirely different Greek word. '*Ekklēsia*' is a completely different word with an entirely different meaning than 'kuriakos.'

Second, reclaim the ontological/semantic particularity of ekklēsia. In the New Testament, the definite article 'the' is never used without qualifying the context, explaining to what particular assembly it is referring to (e.g. 1 Cor 16:19) or to the geographical location of that assembly (e.g. Rom 16:27); ekklēsia is a 'called out' community for a particular purpose or cause in a particular context. Ekklēsia has its location, existence and being within definable geographic limits. Moreover, ekklēsia as living/assembled congregation is plural (1 Cor 15: 4, 12, 19, 23, 28) and thus referring to congregations (Acts 9:31).

Third, re-politicise the original nature and texture of ekklēsia. An ekklēsia was a civil assembly in Athens even before the writing of the New Testament. Ekklēsia was primarily an institution of democracy or a political gathering of competent full citizens of the polis. They met at regular intervals to decide on political and judicial matters. This is reflected three times in the New Testament in Acts 19, the only instances when ekklēsia means 'civil body' or 'town council' in Ephesus (Acts 19:32, 39, 41). Thus, the translators were forced to translate ekklēsia as 'assembly' in these three instances. Therefore, as the feminist theologian Elisabeth Schüssler Fiorenza fittingly defines, ekklēsia is a "radical democratic imagination" and a political hermeneutical space.[33] Ekklēsia signifies a liberative and discursive social space where justice, equality and democracy are practised.

What does διακονία signify then? Literally, διακονία means service (Luke 10:40; 2 Tim. 4:11; Heb. 1:14), relief (Acts 6:1; 11:29; 2 Cor. 8:4), a commission (Acts 12:25; Rom. 15:31) or office in the church (Rom. 12:7; 1 Cor. 12:5; 2 Tim. 4:5). Diakonia also means serving at the table (Acts 6:2). The Bible presents diakonia or service to others as an imperative of Christian discipleship (Mark 10:45). But there is more to the literal meaning of diakonia as ekklēsia is not an institution but a public/democratic/liberative/social space. Such an ekklēsial space cannot be and will not be politically neutral as it demands public interventions and intercessions. Hence diakonia means exercising and embodying the agency of the public space.

This public space is an intersectional space because no space is neutral. As with any social reality, the French philosopher Alain Badiou submits, COVID-19 is an intersection of natural and social determinants.[34] This makes the analysis of the pandemic transversal. Hence, how the pandemic and the downturn permeate people's lifeworlds depend on how the systemic fault lines intersect with issues such as race, ethnicity, the environment, economy, gender, immigration status, etc. It means pandemic-induced issues cannot be solved alone, or else it will be another disaster. It calls for an intersectional approach in our faith response to the pandemic genocide. This best explains why this Council for World Mission study takes on board ecological-economic-ethical issues such as climate change, capitalism, digital imperialism, domestic violence, poverty, migrant issues, grief and loss. It is in understanding faith through the lens of the pandemic and vice versa that we reclaim/reimagine ekklēsia and diakonia in this age of "new normal".

Ekklēsia and diakonia are reciprocally informing and concurrently constitutive. It is often believed that ekklēsia happens first and then diakonia proceeds from it. If so, diakonia becomes the office of the ekklēsia. Instead, it is through diakonia that ekklēsia comes into being, not contrariwise. Diakonia is not derived from or an offshoot of ekklēsia. Nor is it an extension of ekklēsia. Ekklēsia has no ontological or chronological edge over diakonia. The theological basis for both ekklēsia and diakonia is God's plan for the entire created order. Diakonia tells us why there should be ekklēsia. And apart from ekklēsia, diakonia has no meaning; ekklēsia defines and qualifies diakonia.

Ekklēsia is not an eternal entity in time and space, but an event that happens in particular contexts in the life of the people participating in the struggles for freedom, the sanctity of the web of life, human dignity and justice for all. As an event, while disrupting the logic of domination and violence, ekklēsia creates subversive faith communities or "base communities." Then diakonia is the process that makes ekklēsia happen in history. Therefore, it is in responding to COVID-19 through the critical lens of faith and in understanding faith from the vantage point of the virus that we reinvent ekklēsia and diakonia in this age. In doing so, our faith in Jesus makes sense of the material realities in the world.

Endnotes

[1] Charlotte Beale, "Historian Niall Ferguson on what the pandemic means for the global economy, geopolitics - and parties," (29 May 2020). https://www.weforum.org/agenda/2020/05/niall-ferguson-economy-pandemic-coronavirus-covid/

[2] https://www.who.int/dg/speeches/detail/who-director-general-s-opening-remarks-at-the-media-briefing-on-covid-19—11-march-2020

[3] We might call this tendency the "Seneca effect" or the "Seneca cliff," from Lucius Annaeus Seneca who wrote that "increases are of sluggish growth, but the way to ruin is rapid."

[4] "'Economic Viruses Were Already at Work Before Coronavirus': A Conversation with Dr. Cornel West," (11 May 2020). https://www.wnycstudios.org/podcasts/takeaway/segments/conversation-with-cornelwest?fbclid=IwAR1w7Prfebgm1iviyLnVjRUOhmUtmk3HOh4Keeg4UBfmOOdU_HkD1Hiq1Nk

[5] Arundhati Roy, "The pandemic is a portal," (3 April 2020). https://www.ft.com/content/10d8f5e8-74eb-11ea95fefcd274e920ca?fbclid=IwAR2g0kTz4VCKIFeC4CUuxwCIX1afqXyhS90xuf_01fB6qLge6hHUL-nMAH8

[6] Ugo Bardi, "Collapse: The Coronavirus is not a Cause, it is Trigger," 17 April 2020). https://countercurrents.org/2020/04/collapse-the-coronavirus-is-not-a-cause-it-is-a-trigger/

[7] Giorgio Agamben, "The Invention of an Epidemic," (26 Feb 2020). http://www.journal-psychoanalysis.eu/coronavirus-and-philosophers/

[8] Giorgio Shani, "Securitizing 'Bare Life'? Human Security and Coronavirus," 3 April 2020). https://www.e-ir.info/2020/04/03/securitizing-bare-life-human-security-and-coronavirus/?fbclid=IwAR2qNlK1SJl4uDIHQDj9inwAaQPkbEvigWaL_0JMQq39fTTm5WsegpN_Uaw

[9] Interview with Judith Butler, by George Yancy (30 April 2020). https://truthout.org/articles/judith-butler-mourning-is-a-political-act-amid-the-pandemic-and-its-disparities/

[10] Un Report––"COVID-19 and Human Rights: We are all in this together," (20 April 2020). https://www.un.org/sites/un2.un.org/files/un_policy_brief_on_human_rights_and_covid_23_april_2020.pdf, page 10.

[11] https://scroll.in/latest/960045/virus-doesnt-discriminate-its-impacts-do-un-chief-says-covid-19-is-becoming-human-rights-crisis (23 April 2020)

[12] Rebecca Solnot, "Coronavirus does not discriminate, because that's what humans do," (17 April 2020). https://www.theguardian.com/commentisfree/2020/apr/17/coronavirus-discriminate-humans-racism-sexism-inequality

[13] Anmol Ratan, "Covid-19: How Casteist is this Pandemic," (30 April 2020). https://www.justicenews.co.in/covid-19-how-casteist-is-this-pandemic/

[14] Frances Mao, "Coronavirus panic: Why are people stockpiling toilet paper," (4 March 2020). https://www.bbc.com/news/world-australia-51731422

[15] https://twitter.com/GretaThunberg/status/1243579208724557824

[16] https://www.facebook.com/OvergrowTheSystem/posts/1488 704407970938

[17] Arundhati Roy, "The pandemic is a portal," (3 April 2020). https://www. ft.com/content/10d8f5e8-74eb11ea95fefcd274e920ca?fbclid=IwAR2g0kTz4V CKIFeC4CUuxwCIX1afqXyhS90xuf_01fB6qLge6hHUL-nMAH8

[18] Brian Terrell, "Covid-19 and the wasting disease of Normalcy," (20 April 2020). https://www.counterpunch.org/2020/04/20/covid-19-and-the-wasting-disease-of-normalcy/

[19] Slavoj Žižek, *Pandemic!: Covid-19 Shakes the World* (London and New York: OR Books, 2020), 3. The term 'new normal' came into being in the context of 2007-2008 financial crisis. The January 29, 2009, *Philadelphia City Paper* quoted Paul Glover (activist) referring to the need for "new normal" in community development, while introducing his cover story "Prepare for the Best". As of Covid-19, the phrase 'new normal' refers to how pandemic will change daily life for most people.

[20] Niall Ferguson, "Coronavirus: Aids changed us. Will Covid-19 do the same?", (10 May 2020). https://www.thetimes.co.uk/article/coronavirus-aids-changed-us-will-covid-19-do-the-same-bf33h0z9d

[21] Joerg Rieger, "The Ugly Truth of a Pandemic and the Logic of Downturn," (21 May 2020). https://www religionandjustice.org/ blog/faith-needs-labor-to-respond-tothismoment?fbclid=IwAR0_ QXFPReDoMwaRcN19Xz4kCW1o7uaHZRp3hVYmusYB7F7K5s8DluUKw0

[22] Žižek, *Pandemic*, 64.

[23] Willian Strauss and Neil Howe, *The Fourth Turning: An American Prophecy-What the Cycles of History Tell Us About America's Next Rendezvous with Destiny* (New York: Three Rivers Press, 1997).

[24] Plandemic is a 26-minute conspiracy theory video, first posted to social media on May 4, 2020, promoting falsehoods and misinformation about the COVID-19 pandemic.

[25] Asked directly at a press conference whether he had seen evidence that gave him confidence that the Covid-19 emanated from Wuhan lab, President Trump responded "Yes, I have." But he refused to give further details saying "I can't tell you that. I am not allowed to tell you that." But the

US intelligence community said it agreed with the scientific consensus that the virus was not "manmade or genetically modified".

26 Amy Davidson Sorkin, "The Dangerous Coronavirus Conspiracy Theories Targeting 5G Technology, Bill Gates, and a World of Fear," (24 April 2020).

https://www.newyorker.com/news/daily-comment/the-dangerous-coronavirus-conspiracy-theories-targeting-5g-technology-bill-gates-and-a-world-of-fear

27 N. T. Wright, "Christianity Offers No Answers About the Coronavirus. It's Not Supposed To," (29 March 2020). https://time.com/5808495/coronavirus-christianity/

28 William H. Lamar, "It is not just the Coronavirus––bad theology is killing us," (26 May 2020). https://faithandleadership.com/william-h-lamar-iv-its-not-just-coronavirus-bad-theology-killing-us?fbclid=IwAR0W0ISU3RpwfoZmE6-YcraQjiWaGOjEdz_rNdekkrWxnyKKNAstE7Ma9yg

29 Cameron Doddy, (13 March 2020). https://novenanews.com/bishop-blasts-providentialist-catholics-coronavirus/

30 https://www.facebook.com/Nazarenes4Peace/photos/a.131593074849286 8/3411106158975306/?type=3&theater

31 The word ekklēsia is wrongly translated as 'church' 112 times and rendered it as 'assembly' three times in the New Testament. In Acts 19, *ekklēsia* is a civil body in Ephesus. Thus, the translators were forced to abandon their fake translation in these three instances. 'Matthew's Bible' (1537) and The Great Bible (1539) also retained Tyndale's translation (1526) of *ekklēsia as 'congregation'*. However, the Geneva Bible (1557), and later Bishops' Bible (1568) was the first to translate *ekklēsia* as 'church'.

32 Herbert Gordon May, *Our English Bible in the Making* (Philadelphia: Westminister, 1952), 49–50.

33 Elisabeth Sch sssler Fiorenza, *The Power of the Word: Scripture and Rhetoric of Empire* (Minneapolis: Fortress, 2007), 70–71.

34 Alain Badiou, "On the Epidemic Situation," (23 March 2020). https://www.versobooks.com/blogs/4608-on-the-epidemic-situation

Chapter 1

Pandemic or Planetdemic?: Ecology of Disease and Planetary Health

Nature sustains us. It's where we originated. The lesson for humanity from this pandemic is not to be afraid of nature, but rather to restore it, embrace it, and understand how to live with and benefit from it…. The wise way forward is to invest in conservation and science, and to embrace nature and the glorious variety of life with which we share this planet. A healthy future for humanity and a healthy biodiverse planet go hand in hand.

Thomas E. Lovejoy

Pandemics are on the rise, and we need to contain the process that drives them, not just the individual diseases. Plagues are not only part of our culture; they are caused by it…spillovers of diseases from animals to humans are increasing exponentially as our ecological footprint brings us closer to wildlife in remote areas and the wildlife trade brings these animals into urban centers. Unprecedented road-building, deforestation, land clearing and agricultural development, as well as globalized travel and trade, make us supremely susceptible to pathogens like coronaviruses. COVID-19 is fundamentally a story of humanity's ever-encroaching relationship with all other living things on this planet.

Emma Gilchrist

Introduction

After closing down at the onset of the coronavirus pandemic, Barcelona's Gran Teatre del Liceu opera house reopened on 22 June 2020 with its first concert to an atypical audience of 2,292 potted plants filling the seats. This unique concert was organised a day after Spain lifted its coronavirus lockdown. The event was the work of conceptual artist Eugenio Ampudia to examine our relationship with nature and the impact the lockdown has had on public spaces. The UceLi Quartet performed Puccini's 1890 movement Crisantemi ("Chrysanthemums"). After the concert, all the plants were to be donated to healthcare professionals working on the frontlines against the virus. The famed opera house said in a statement that following this "strange, painful period," organisers wanted to "offer us a different perspective for our return to activity, a perspective that brings us closer to something as essential as our relationship with nature." This challenges people and faith communities not only to curb COVID-19 in an eco-friendly manner but also to reimagine a post-COVID world and its "ecosystem services."

Ecology of the Pandemic

In the view of American linguist and political philosopher Noam Chomsky, Brazilian liberation theologian Leonardo Boff and climate economist Gernot Wagner, COVID-19 must be attributed to human-induced climate change at warp speed, calamitous loss of biodiversity and reckless encroachment on natural habitat or wild land.[1] Scientists identify such an era as an age of humans or 'anthropocene.' Joerg Rieger, on other hand, argues that it is not anthropocene but 'capitalocene' era. He defines capitalocene thus: "Maybe it is not 'anthropocene'—you know, humanity, as such—but it is certain forces that humans have created ... a way of exploiting nature, which surprisingly really resembles how we're exploiting human beings."[2]

According to a UN Environment Programme (UNEP) report, "This demonstrates a trade-off between consumption-driven society (and its interference with nature) and the resiliency of nature and ecosystems. Regardless of its cause or origin, the emergence of COVID-19 has underscored the mutually-affective and dysfunctional relationship between people and nature."[3] The Intergovernmental Science Policy Platform on Biodiversity and Ecosystem Services (IPBES) categorically states: "There is a single species that is responsible for the COVID-19 pandemic—us."[4] This explains why there are discussions about 'green recovery' in relation to the post-pandemic world.

If we look back in time, there is a common link between pandemic outbreaks and severe climate phenomena like El Niño. The National Oceanic and Atmospheric Administration of the United States defines "the El Niño/Southern Oscillation (ENSO) as a natural climate phenomenon that causes anomalous interannual climate variability patterns driven by changes in wind and surface ocean temperatures across the Equatorial Pacific Ocean, affecting mostly the areas of the tropics and the subtropics." The ENSO has a significant impact not only on the earth's ecosystems but also on human societies. Two major components of this phenomenon are the El Niño and the La Niña weather patterns, each representing the extreme warming phase and the extreme cooling phase of sea surface temperature over the Pacific Ocean, respectively. During El Nino events, severe droughts, floods and even deadly wildfires like the ones that raged in the Amazon occur all over the world. Ironically, the pandemic outburst in December occurred when climate variations were brewing in the Equatorial Pacific.

Year 2019 was one of the hottest in the last decade, spurred on by an extreme El Niño event which resulted in an increase in rainfall patterns, threatened rice crops and intensified air pollution in China. This meteorological phenomenon, through the generation of weak winds, facilitated the transfer of moisture from southern to northern China. Besides, it is known that a very humid atmosphere enhances the retention of polluting particles in the atmosphere, which may have 'carried' the virus and contributed to its airborne transmission. A sun that 'cooks us' (global warming) drives the extreme El Niño phenomena that lead to hydrological alterations, which in turn contribute to various waterborne and vector-borne diseases with the bloom of pathogens. It is considered that during droughts, remnant stagnant water allows insect vectors to increase their populations, and flooding and soil moisture extend their reproduction periods. As the World Economic Forum states:

> Natural habitats are being reduced, causing species to live in closer quarters than ever to one another and to humans. As some people opt to invade forests and wild landscapes due to business interests and others at the other end of the socioeconomic spectrum are forced to search for resources for survival, we damage the ecosystems, risking that viruses from animals find new hosts—us.[5]

Therefore, humans may become infected either directly through infected animals' bites or saliva (zoonotic transmission) or indirectly via vectors (which serve as an intermediate host) that carry the disease pathogens and transmit it while biting humans.[6] In the case of COVID-19, scientists suggest that the outbreak of the pandemic occurred through zoonotic transmission associated with a large seafood market in Wuhan, which was followed by human-to-human transmission. And therefore, we suddenly realise how climatic phenomena can trigger deadly and debilitating diseases affecting various aspects of human life, health, the practice of medicine, politics, economy and even evolution:

> Climate change is also a driver of zoonoses. Greenhouse gas emissions—primarily the result of burning fossil fuels—cause changes in temperature and humidity, which directly affects the survival of microbes. Rapid changes to habitat due to unusual weather events such as heat, drought, flooding or wildfires are too rapid to allow ecosystems to balance sudden spikes in populations of group species such as mosquitoes, which can be vectors for emerging diseases.[7]

The UNEP officially confirmed that COVID-19 is a zoonotic disease that can transmit between animals and humans just like SARS (2002), Avian Influenza or bird flu (2004), H1N1 or Swine Flu (2009), Middle East Respiratory Syndrome or MERS (2012), Ebola (2014-2015), Zika virus (2015-2016) and the West Nile virus (2019).[8] Almost a century's worth of global trends confirm that the 'spillover' of disease from animals to human is occurring more frequently than earlier. In his new book, *How to Survive a Pandemic*, American physician Michael Greger states that "from tuberculosis to bird flu and HIV to coronavirus, these infectious diseases share a common origin story: human interaction with animals." According to the 2016 UNEP report, 75 per cent of all emerging infectious diseases in humans are now zoonotic as their origin is wildlife and domesticated animals.[9] Ignoring such a strong warning about the dystopian hellscape that awaits us would be a "dangerous delusion," Chomsky has said.[10] Compared with the lethal consequences of the coronavirus pandemic, climate change is a 'silent killer' as the effects of climate change seem to be moving slower, because of which we disregard the negative repercussions of it. [11] It is predicted that the dreadful impact of climate change would create a scenario even more dangerous than that of COVID-19.

COVID-19 is a compelling proof of how closely the planet's health and pandemics are linked. The World Economic Forum states, "Just as carbon is not the cause of climate change, it is human activity—not nature—that causes many pandemics."[12] Any attempt therefore to find solutions to convalesce from the crisis must take the 'ecology of the pandemic' as its method and basis; "COVID-19 and nature are linked. So should be the recovery."[13] And the recent Seychelles' marine-protection initiative offers us hope that if every country does its part, the planet can be safer and healthier. In other words, the decision we make on how to respond to the coronavirus pandemic will impact the future health of people and the planet, and a poor response would be detrimental to the survival of the human species itself; "nature is our best antiviral." But strategies to mitigate COVID-19 have led to another ecological crisis due to the increased use of single-use disposable face masks and latex gloves around the world.

'COVID Waste' and 'Plastic nightmares'

The Copernicus Climate Change Service (C3S) and the Copernicus Atmosphere Monitoring Service (CAMS) by the European Centre for Medium-Range Weather Forecasts (ECMWF) reported that a hole one million square kilometres wide in the ozone layer above the Arctic had closed/healed.[14] It was noticed in March 2020 and was thought to be due to the unusual atmospheric conditions thanks to the reduced levels of pollution. Believed to be the largest hole in the ozone layer, it would have led to a bigger threat had it moved towards the south. The ECMWF added that the closing of the hole was not due to the reduced levels of pollution during the coronavirus lockdown. It is believed that the polar vortex, the high-altitude currents that are responsible for bringing cold air to the polar regions, was responsible for the healing of the layer.

While environmentalists have appreciated the reduction in pollution due to lockdowns enforced across the world by many nations, the spotlight will soon be on global medical waste treatment management. Wearing a face mask has become the new normal. But disposable face masks and gloves are a plastics nightmare. Take the case of Wuhan. The Chinese city, the epicentre of the pandemic and home to over 11 million people, is reported to have generated 200 tonnes of clinical trash on a single day (24 February 2020)—four times the city's only dedicated facility can incinerate per day.[15] The visible rise in the usage of single-use face masks, bottles of sanitisers and disposable gloves that will eventually end up in landfills and water sources will result in a new environmental issue, the so-called 'mask pollution.' Laurent Lombard from the French non-profit organisation Mer Propre says, "Soon we'll run the risk of having more masks than jellyfish in the Mediterranean."[16]

Environmental group Oceans Asia conducted a survey trip to the Soko Islands in Hong Kong, where it found surgical masks washing up on the shoreline. These marine debris or COVID waste—especially single-use masks typically made from plastics like polypropylene, a fossil fuel-derived plastic that can take hundreds of years to break down, and disposable gloves that are not biodegradable—are an ecological timebomb given their lasting detrimental impact on the planet. Medical waste is typically incinerated after use due to public health reasons, contributing to greenhouse gas emissions—although other options, such as disinfecting the waste before recycling it, are possible. According to a World Wildlife Fund (WWF) report, incorrect disposal of even 1 per cent of the masks pose a huge threat.[17]

Green Recovery from the Pandemic

Has bicycle got anything to do with COVID-19? Can bicycles be a solution to the challenges of the post-COVID recovery? These questions might sound weird and funny. But many raised these questions when they saw an article by the Department of Global Communications on the UN website posted on 22 May 2020—"United Nations eyes bicycles as driver of post-COVID-19 'green recovery.'"[18] According to UN reports, "European member countries of the United Nations recently created a task force to take this question further and discuss ways to make post-COVID-19 mobility more environmentally sound, healthy and sustainable." The United Nations Economic Commission for Europe (UNECE) see the coronavirus pandemic as an opportunity and obligation for the transport sector to restart in a manner that is conducive to a more efficient, greener system; it states that "a 'new normal' needs to be developed to replace 'business as usual.'"

Responding to these trends, Bonn, Dublin, Brussels and Milan have urged the European Commission—the executive branch of the European Union—for a multibillion euro grant scheme for zero-emission public transport. While outlining Europe's 'green recovery' plan from the COVID-19 crisis, EU Commission President Ursula von der Leyen promised the European Parliament that the Green Deal would be at the centre of the EU's recovery effort.[19] Many countries and cities are focusing on micro-mobility, in favour of cyclists and pedestrians, in their response to the COVID pandemic. The mayor of Athens,

Kostas Bakoyannis, announced plans to allocate 50,000 square metres of public space for cyclists and pedestrians. At the heart of the scheme will be a four-mile "grand walkway" uniting archaeological sites in the historic centre. Berlin, Budapest and Paris set up pop-up bike lanes across the city.

Brands such as Collina Strada are exploring more eco-friendly options and making cloth masks out of deadstock or leftover materials. According to experts, reusable cloth masks—which should be washed at 60 degree Celsius to kill the virus—are just as effective when it comes to stopping the spread of COVID-19 in non-medical settings. "[For] the person on the street, the cloth masks are perfectly adequate," says Dr Jane Greatorex, a virologist at the University of Cambridge. Scientists are also looking at more eco-friendly alternatives to the medical masks currently on the market, with researchers at the University of British Columbia developing a biodegradable mask made of wood fibres. Bioplastics (made from natural materials) is another potential alternative, although the unique properties of surgical masks, which prevent the virus from getting through, are difficult to recreate. The pandemic has undoubtedly shone a spotlight on the problem, meaning we could see more sustainable and greener solutions sooner rather than later.

In order to tackle the huge environmental impact of COVID waste and mask pollution, there are many initiatives in India too as elsewhere in the world. Delhi-based professor Joginder Singh, who is the head of the research department at Gateway Education, made a range of low-cost devices such as Automatic Sanitiser Dispenser, Automatic Sanitising Tunnels and Automatic Foot Sanitising Machine. He donated these machines to police stations and small hospitals where masks are used at a much higher frequency.[20] The Noida Authority (near Delhi) initiated efforts to dispose of used masks scientifically. The staff of the agency appointed by the authority for sanitation work will collect such waste from each household.[21]

'Eco-Casteism': Caste and Ecological Politics in India

Indian environmental movements have been vibrant in articulating the voices of women, tribal communities, the poor, marginal, vulnerable and displaced people, environmental refugees and migrants. However, when it comes to questions of caste and Dalit positions on ecological politics, there appears to be an 'environmental blindness'. Though Dalits have often participated in various significant environmental movements, they have been missing as a category in studies because they are usually identified in the general categories of the poor, marginal people, refugees and migrants. The Dalit environmental public space is often outside the ambit of the dominant environmental discursive frame. While problematising the seeming invisibility of Dalit issues in mainline Indian environmentalism, Dalit perspectives challenge the construction of a partial environmental politics which is often Brahminical and reinforces a deeply entrenched Hindu conservatism. More importantly, Dalit images and symbols illuminate the ecological sensibility of marginal communities and colonised constituencies. The works of anti-caste intellectuals like B.R. Ambedkar, Periyar E.V. Ramasamy and Jyotiba Phule offer insightful critiques of caste-blind Brahminical environmentalism.

Dalit environmentalism attempts to weave together the issues of caste, gender, labour, human rights, food, land, human dignity, water and occupation to explore the intersection of Dalit issues and environmentalism. Gail Omvedt's article, "Why Dalits Dislike Environmentalists?" (1997), points to the disconnect between two of the most powerful social movements in India—the anti-caste movement and the ecological movement. The Indian political theorist Kancha Ilaiah refers to Indian environmentalism as exclusive and insensitive to the existential and ontological concerns of the builders of the environment.[22] Dalit perspectives on ecology cannot afford to overlook its intersectionality with environmentalism because villages, food, water, agriculture, land and irrigation have been important sites of colonisation and imposition of caste hegemony; a caste economy thrives on the use and abuse of natural resources.

Planetary Civilisation and Reimagining Human

Emergent pandemic diseases are anthropogenic diseases—caused by human activities and not natural disasters. As Vandana Shiva rightly puts it, "Human greed, with no respect for the rights of other species or even for our fellow human beings, is at the root of this pandemic and future pandemics."[23] The COVID-19 pandemic has reminded us in a devastating way of the interconnected nature of economy, the environment, human health; "everything on our planet is interconnected—and we are part of the equation."[24] Leonardo Boff strongly argues that the coronavirus pandemic demands "a different relationship with nature and the Earth. If after the crisis has passed, we don't make the necessary changes, the next time may be the last, since we will have become staunch enemies of the Earth. And she may no longer want us here."[25]

We cannot continue to have the dangerous illusion of mastery of nature and become the reason for the next pandemic. And finally, to extinction. American author Eileen Crist argues that the techno-managerial "portfolio—which would include such initiatives as climate geoengineering, desalination, de-extinction, and off-planet colonization—is in keeping with the social rubric of human distinction."[26] The pandemic will not only change human life but also raise some important questions about the emergence of a new human being in the post-COVID world, argues the Moroccan politician Iliyas El Omari.[27] This calls for a post-pandemic reimagination of the 'human being,' which will be and have to be different from the pre-pandemic generation.

As the "earth is in the throes of a mass extinction event and climate change upheaval," any attempt to signify 'ekklēsia' and 'diakonia' in the context of COVID-19 must take as its vantage point planetary shifts, the stark reminders of ecological predicament and the possible environmental measures to be taken to avert the next pandemic. Like all other fatal emergencies in the past, COVID has also undeniably proved human beings' 'Promethean' impulse, to be masters of nature and manipulate, exploit and control other species as objects for profit. Human beings are not separate from nature. "The Earth will continue to evolve, with or without us."[28] This compels the new ekklēsia and diakonia in the post-pandemic matrix to reimagine a human that no longer identifies with speciesism.

Radical environmentalist philosopher Derrick Jensen, in his impassionate polemic *The Myth of Human Supremacy*, debunks one of culture's most pernicious and nature-devouring myth, that of human supremacy. In this much-necessary and provocative book, Jensen dissects suicidal impulses that constitute the human craving for dominance and the fatal belief in progress that triggers ecocide. To problematise the paralysis of conventional science and technology, he explores the complexities, intelligence and sentience of all other beings than human. Only by destroying the sociopathy of our consciousness as the 'anointed species' will we be able to save ourselves and our planet. The world as an interconnected web of beings call for demythologising the "hegemonic human being." Boff makes it categorical: "There is no escape. Either we recognise ourselves as humans—co-equal in the same Common Home—or we will all sink."[29]

The book of Genesis is often interpreted as providing a justification for the exploitation of nature. In Genesis, God considers the creation of humans and says, "Let us make humankind in our image, according to our likeness; and let them have dominion over the fish of the sea, and over the birds of the air, and over the cattle, and over all the wild animals of the earth, and over every creeping thing that creeps upon the earth" (Gen 1:26). Lynn White points explicitly to this rule of humanity over the rest of creation as responsible for a Christian attitude that denigrates the importance of nature. This "imperial and anti-ecological anthropology" seems to be implied in the Christian doctrine of the *imago dei*, humans created in the image of God.

According to the Old Testament scholar Walter Brueggemann, the Old Testament does not portray human beings as autonomous.[30] Brueggemann has said that being made in God's image means that humans are created to rule over creation "in the way that God ruled over creation." He contends that Old Testament humans are understood as being situated in the same transactional processes with the holiness of Yahweh, as in Israel ("covenantal notions of personhood"). The phrase *imago dei* (Gen 1:27) basically refers to those characteristics of human beings that make communication with God possible and enable them to take up God-given responsibilities outlined in Genesis 1:28. As the author and source of life, God shares not only his image but also his very life and glory with the created order (Psalms 19). Here we are reminded that creation may not be *creatio ex nihilo* (creation out of nothing), but rather *creatio ex profundis* (creation out of the deep waters, creation as the germinating abyss). Creation thus participates in the life of the creator. God is biologically present in all of creation and hence God's family includes the whole cosmos.

The Old Testament theological notion of the entire humanity sharing the responsibility of 'ruling' over God's creation is a political/anti-imperial/anti-monarchic polemic critiquing a function otherwise exclusively linked to emperors and kings. Genesis 1:26–28 also challenges the characteristic association of "the image of God" with Mesopotamian or Persian kings and Egyptian pharaohs. In this respect, as Mark Brett argues, God's creation of humanity in the image of God democratises an ancient Near Eastern royal usage of image language; all human beings are created in the image of God, not just kings/emperors/pharaohs.[31] The result is that all interhuman hierarchical understandings are set aside; all human beings of whatever station in life stand together as image of God. It rejects all essentialist notions of human personhood; thus human person is to be understood in relational, and not essentialist, ways.

However, the idea that humanity is made in the image of God is actually not very dominant in the Old Testament as one would think. The other place in the Old Testament where a similar idea is expressed, linked with a strong statement about humanity's dominion over the earth, is in Psalms 8:5–6 ("Thou hast made him a little lower than God, and dost crown him with glory and majesty! Thou dost make him to rule over the works of Thy hands; Thou hast put all things under his feet.") Keith Carley, also writing in the Earth Bible series, argues that this Psalm represents "an apology for human domination" that does not conform to eco-justice principles.

"Image of God" is not self-contained, self-sufficient and static as if God is an asocial reality. It implies that the fullness of humanity is shared, participatory and reciprocal. In the words of Brueggemann, Genesis 2–3 provides two images of God: *potter* and *farmer/gardener*. God as a *potter* (Gen 2:7) is "hands on" with the craft. It has often been noted that the verb form (*ysr*) as it pertains to creation is not by dictum, but by actual engagement with the raw stuff out of which the object is formed. The transition from *dominus* (owner) to *frater* (brother/sister) underscores human dependence *on* the rest of creation and not human domination *over* the earth.

According to George Zachariah, Genesis 2–3 would have emerged from an agrarian community. Zachariah argues that "the vision of humanity that emerged from a farming community—a community of ecological and social relations of solidarity and communion which is antithetical to the logical of an imperial exploitative system—is that of a dependent and responsible member of the ecosystem with the vocation to farmers."[32] This green image of God with his hands in the dirt is remarkable; this is no naïve theology, but a statement about the depths to which God has entered into the life of creation. God's very life is then breathed into human; something of God's own self becomes an integral part of the human identity, enabling life to move from God out into the larger world.

God is also imaged as a *farmer/gardener*, placing two trees in this garden; they are associated with life and death and the related human choices (Deut 30:15–20). Yahweh as *gardener* is often the subject of the verb plant. In Isaiah 5:1–2 in particular, the gardener-vinedresser is involved in the founding of the garden and in creating the best possible vineyard. ("Let me sing for my beloved my love-song concerning his vineyard: My beloved had a vineyard on a very fertile hill. He dug it and cleared it of stones, and planted it with choice vines; he built a watchtower in the midst of it, and hewed out a wine vat in it; he expected it to yield grapes, but it yielded wild grapes" —Isa 5:1-2 NRSV). Hence, the primary responsibility of human beings created in the "green image of God" is ecological.

Conclusion

A radical ecological conversion challenges the conventional anthropocentric understanding of ekklēsia and diakonia, which is rooted in human being's supremacy and self-referentiality. The word ekklēsia literally means "called out"; here the question is called 'from' what and called 'to' what. Is God's calling an ontological human prerogative? What about 'all creation' other than human beings? God has created all species with an intention or purpose. The purpose of creation is not something that a species arrives at a later stage. Purpose and creation cannot be separated in terms of chronology. If so, God's purpose of creation is God's calling. This inherent vocation of all species de-privileges human beings.

All created species are interconnected and thus participate in the calling/purpose and the principles of the shared breath of life. If God's calling is not different from the purpose of creation, then *klesis* (calling) should not be taken as 'separated' in a privileged/ontological/biological sense. As opposed to *creatio ex nihilo*, which assumes that evil is disorder and not unjust order, Catherine Keller proposes *creatio ex profundis*. Keller's *tehomopholic* non-anthropocentric idea of creation suggests the agency of all species. 'Calling' means 'to be' in the web of life and thus experience fullness of life in this relationship. This calls for a new way of being a faith community (ekklēsia) in relation to the earth (eco-metanoia) and its bio-history—ecoklesia/bioklesia.

Not just ekklēsia alone, practising diakonia ecologically is also vital in the face of COVID-19. By unsettling the rhizomatic layers of planetary interdependence and colonising the commons, we subvert God's creation and its biorhythm. An unsparing autopsy of the coronavirus would expose the truth that it is the abuse of wild animals and the systemic and consistent disdain for environmental protocols that caused the outbreak. The coronavirus pandemic is a zoonotic disease. Hence, diakonia in the age of the pandemic means participating in the mutual web of life wherein different organisms of life sustain each other—ecodiakonia; in Keller's words, ecodiakonia means "creative collaboration with nature."[33] This co-participation with nature as green ethical beings may be realised through compassion, coexistence and cooperation. It implies de-privileging and decolonising human agency. Such a befitting non-anthropocentric faith response to the pandemic could be achieved, as George Zachariah rightly points out, by being an "ally of ecojustice struggles" and through "inter-faith collisions." In pursuing the latter, ecodiakonia/biodiakonia can draw on Buddhist traditions and notions of ecodharma, and other evolving ecological paradigms such as 'agroecology.'

<u>Preamble, A People's Manifesto for Ecological Democracy</u>[34]

Our planet is not a lump of inanimate matter circling the sun every year, providing humans free lodging, boarding and endless resources to exploit recklessly. She is a living, breathing, sentient Being, to be treated with love, care and deep respect. Revered in all ancient cultures around the world as Pachamama, Gaia, Bhumi or Mother Earth—She gives us generously but her respect needs to be earned too.

Humans, even though they pretend to dominate it, are not 'masters' of the planet. We are not mysteriously destined to rule over all other species—whether plants, animals or microbes. Humans, like every other living organism, are the children of

Mother Earth and just one out of millions of other forms of life. And it is the ability to coexist peacefully amidst immense diversity, that makes all life itself possible.

The quest for endless and ruthless domination of everything around us is at the root cause of our historical downfall, because we do unto others within our species, what we do unto members of other species. Much before the exploitation of humans by humans, came the exploitation of Nature by humans. The idea of colonisation of Mother Earth has to be defeated in order to truly end the colonial domination of race, caste, gender and wealth within human societies.

The source of all spirituality, over the millennia, has been the awe-inspiring beauty and compassion of our planet as well as the deeply humbling realization of the ephemeral and transient nature of human life. There is a need today to recover our lost spirituality by connecting back with Mother Earth and all its life forms, not just for the sake of the planet but for our own survival and salvation.

Are human beings redeemable at all? Yes, of course they are. Humans are the only creatures on the planet, who look after, not just their young, but also their elderly, sick and disabled members. Humans are in other words, at their finest, when they fight against injustice or show solidarity and empathy towards each other, especially the weakest in their midst. It is these noble qualities, of an otherwise flawed species, that need to be preserved and nurtured at all costs, in all that we do. They are the only source of hope for our future.

Endnotes

[1] Interview with Noam Chomsky, by Jipson John and Jithesh P. M. https://thewire.in/world/noam-chomsky-interview-covid-19-pandemic-capitalism-neoliberalism-us-hegemony.

[2] https://www.facebook.com/535944740227752/posts/872545249901031/

[3] Interview with Pushpam Kumar, Chief Environmental Economist, UNEP. https://www.unenvironment.org/news-and-stories/story/covid-19-and-nature-trade-paradigm

⁴ Josef Settele, Sandra Díaz and Eduardo Brondizio and Dr. Peter Daszak, "COVID-19 Stimulus Measures Must Save Lives, Protect Livelihoods, and Safeguard Nature to Reduce the Risk of Future Pandemics," (27 April 2020). https://ipbes.net/covid19stimulus

⁵ Marie Quinney, "COVID-19 and nature are linked. So should be the recovery," (14 April 2020). https://www.weforum.org/agenda/2020/04/covid-19-nature-deforestation-recovery/

⁶ Žižek, *Pandemic*, 89.

⁷ https://www.unenvironment.org/news-and-stories/story/science-points-causes-covid-19 (22 May 2020).

⁸ "Science points to causes of COVID-19," (22 May 2020). https://www.unenvironment.org/news-and-stories/story/science-points-causes-covid-19

⁹ "Emerging zoonotic diseases and links to ecosystem health – UNEP Frontiers 2016 chapter," (8 April 2020). https://www.unenvironment.org/resources/emerging-zoonotic-diseases-and-links-ecosystem-health-unep-frontiers-2016-chapter

¹⁰ Interview with Noam Chomsky, by Jipson John and Jithesh P. M. https://thewire.in/world/noam-chomsky-interview-covid-19-pandemic-capitalism-neoliberalism-us-hegemony.

¹¹ Chris Sasaki, "'A silent killer': U of T's Miriam Diamond on what COVID-19 has taught us about climate change," (6 May 2020). https://www.utoronto.ca/news/silent-killer-u-t-s-miriam-diamond-what-covid-19-has-taught-us-about-climate-change

¹² Marie Quinney, "COVID-19 and nature are linked. So should be the recovery," (14 April 2020). https://www.weforum.org/agenda/2020/04/covid-19-nature-deforestation-recovery/

¹³ Marie Quinney, "COVID-19 and nature are linked. So should be the recovery," (14 April 2020). https://www.weforum.org/agenda/2020/04/covid-19-nature-deforestation-recovery/

¹⁴ ECMWF added that the closing of the hole was not due to the reduced levels of pollution during the coronavirus lockdown. It is believed that the polar vortex, the high-altitude currents that are responsible for bringing cold air to the polar regions, is responsible for the healing of the layer.

¹⁵ Suchetana Mukhopadhyay, "COVID-19: Unmasking the Environmental Impact," (20 March 2020). https://earth.org/covid-19-unmasking-the-environmental-impact/

[16]   Ashifa Kassam, "'More masks than jellyfish': coronavirus waste ends up in ocean," (8 June 2020).

https://www.theguardian.com/environment/2020/jun/08/more-masks-than-jellyfish-coronavirus-waste-ends-up-in-ocean

[17] "Responsibility is required when disposing of masks and gloves" (29 April 2020). https://www.wwf.it/scuole/?53500%2FNello-smaltimento-di-mascherine-e-guanti-serve-responsabilita

[18] "UN eyes bicycles as driver of post-COVID-19 'green recovery,'" (22 May 2020). https://www.un.org/en/coronavirus/un-eyes-bicycles-driver-post-covid-19-%E2%80%98green-recovery%E2%80%99

[19] Frédéric Simon, "LEAKED: Europe's draft 'green recovery' plan," (21 May 2020). https://www.euractiv.com/section/energy-environment/news/leaked-europes-draft-green-recovery-plan/?utm_content=1589963397&utm_medium=EURACTIV&utm_source=twitter

[20] Aprajita Sharad, "World Environment Day 2020: Stop the mask pollution, urge environmentalists," (5 June 2020). https://www.hindustantimes.com/more-lifestyle/world-environment-day-2020-stop-the-mask-pollution-urge-environmentalists/story-pxjhhjoN3zYMIqZK21X82N.html

[21] Vinod Rajput, "Don't throw away used masks, hand them over to waste collectors for proper disposal," 10 April 2020). https://www.hindustantimes.com/noida/don-t-throw-away-used-masks-hand-them-over-to-waste-collectors-for-proper-disposal/story-wZEWbaM0qSmIKuPa7U3EZP.html

[22] Kancha Ilaiah, *Post-Hindu India: A Discourse in Dalit-Bahujan, Socio-Spiritual and Scientific Revolution* (New Delhi, SAGE, 2009),140—158.

[23] Vandana Shiva, "A virus, humanity, and the earth," (5 April 2020). https://www.deccanherald.com/specials/sunday-spotlight/a-virus-humanity-and-the-earth-821527.html

[24] "Everything on our planet is interconnected - and we are part of the equation," 22 May 2020). https://updates.panda.org/interconnected

[25]   Mada Jurado (26 March 2020). https://novenanews.com/theologian-coronavirus-different-relationship-earth/?fbclid=IwAR0icJ-fyG3TZYF6MNP_Sym_F6BXZPnXkB2oMUfnxh31SFmNW2WQj4p1IXM

[26]   Eileen Crist, "Reimagining Human," (14 December 2018). https://science.sciencemag.org/content/362/6420/1242

[27] Ilyas El Omari, "A new human being will emerge in the post-Covid-19 world," (8 April 2020).

https://www.orfonline.org/expert-speak/a-new-human-being-will-emege-in-the-post-covid-19-world-64275/

28   Vandana Shiva, "A virus, humanity, and the earth," (5 April 2020). https://www.deccanherald.com/specials/sunday-spotlight/a-virus-humanity-and-the-earth-821527.html

29   Mada Jurado (26 March 2020). https://novenanews.com/theologian-coronavirus-different-relationship-earth/?fbclid=IwAR0icJ-fyG3TZYF6MNP_Sym_F6BXZPnXkB2oMUfnxh31SFmNW2WQj4p1IXM

30 Walter Brueggemann, *Genesis* (Atlanta: John Knox Press, 1982), 32.

31 Mark Brett, *Genesis: Procreation and Politics of Identity* (London and NY: Routledge, 2000), 28.

32 George Zachariah, *Gospel in a Groaning World: Climate Justice and Public Witness* (NCCI/CSS: Thiruvalla, 2012), 66. See also Claus Westermann, *Creation* (translated by John J. Scullion; London: SPCK, 1971), 81-82.

33 Catherine Keller, "A Letter from Catherine Keller," (2 April 2020). https://medium.com/@dostlund_42808/a-letter-from-catherine-keller-1930029c4914

34 "Preamble, A People's Manifesto for Ecological Democracy," (15 April 2020). https://countercurrents.org/2020/08/a-peoples-manifesto-for-ecological-democracy/?fbclid=IwAR2QW3-YmSj9ryfVQNINiG2sz23rBvgog6QvzFjcDo232CatQrPwVw5BHqQ

Chapter 2

Economic Holocaust and Pandemic Capitalism

The two greatest crops on earth are hunger and thirst.

P. Sainath

Our citizens work hard, but solely with the object of getting rich. Their chief interest is commerce, and their chief aim in life is, as they call it, 'doing business.'

Albert Camus, *The Plague*

Introduction

Everybody Loves a Good Drought (1996) by Palagummi Sainath is perhaps an established classic on rural India. While making a scathing indictment of the elite, Sainath pithily highlights the 'two Indias' in the country. One might wonder if there was a marketing gimmick behind the book's title. But it was not Sainath's idea. A peasant activist from Jharkhand, a state in eastern India, had wryly remarked how drought reliefs are a bonanza—*teesri fasal*, meaning third crop—for the administrative and political machinery, NGOs, multilateral agencies, the media, contractors and the so-called intellectuals. What he meant was the bigger the calamity, the larger was the cut of the budget for work sanctioned and hence all of them loved a good flood or a drought. It is an opportunity for those who have political power and unbridled access to natural resources to exploit any misery—be it natural or human-induced—for monetary and political benefit. It is an 'opportunity' for crony capitalist forces to further open up and loot economies. If so, it is indisputably possible that corporates and capitalists would seize the COVID-19 pandemic as a chance to extend their economic reach and negotiating power.

Seven of the top global consultancy firms—Bain & Co, EY, PwC, BCG, KPMG, Primus Partners and Mirae Asset Management—have already joined hands with 'Invest India' to chalk out an economic revival strategy for India after the pandemic ends to make this "a watershed period" attracting foreign investments. The pandemic has also demonstrated the efficacy of employing pertinent technology. This also opens a lot of opportunities for tech giants and capital firms. Google is investing $4.5 billion for a 7.73 per cent stake in India's Jio Platforms. By the end of 2020, Google plans to enable one million teachers and 22,000 schools across India with free online tools like G-Suite, Google Classroom and YouTube in classrooms. India, with its strong domestic demand, is where everybody wants to be during this pandemic.

With the rising demand for online platforms that deliver grocery and household essentials, JioMart has started outlets in 200 cities in India. BigBasket and Grofers, India's biggest online grocers, have nearly doubled the number of daily deliveries. Similar to its food service, Zomato now also has the option of 'contactless' grocery shopping. It has diversified into the grocery business and is now delivering in over 80 cities in India. PhonePe, a digital payments app, has launched a new feature that enables home delivery of essentials while ensuring 'contactless' payment. Corporates and capitalists definitely like a 'good pandemic' for sure.

COVID-19 Spillover and Capitalism

Apart from being one of the biggest killers, COVID-19 has devastated global economies. According to International Monetary Fund reports, "It is already clear, however, that global growth will turn sharply negative in 2020…we now project that over 170 countries will experience *negative* per capita income growth this year" (emphasis original).[1] Pandemic-related disruptions have led to unemployment. In the US alone, 963,000 people filed for claims in the first week of August 2020.[2] Retail stores are especially hit. Now a 'restaurant apocalypse' is under way as the industry is being hit fiercely. We are also facing the quickest and deepest oil demand crash in history. Oil prices plunged to an inconceivable negative $37.63 a barrel as on 21 April 2020 as global fossil fuel demand dropped roughly 30 per cent.[3] The decline in oil prices has also put a downward pressure on the prices for palm oil, soybean oil, sugar and corn.

According to Noam Chomsky, the pandemic has only exposed the deep-rooted "suicidal tendencies" of capitalist logic and "the savage neoliberal variant of capitalism."[4] Obviously, as economists like Mariana Mazzucato believe, this should reshape the economy to become more inclusive and sustainable, with the state playing more of a role. The reality, however, is "entrenchment of the prevailing system" of dispossession and dependency.[5] On 20 April 2020, the *Wall Street Journal* reported that "scores of countries are asking for bailouts and loans from financial institutions with $1.2 trillion to lend. An ideal recipe for fuelling dependency."[6] Chomsky predicted this would be not impossible. "The beneficiaries of the savage capitalism of the past 40 years of neoliberalism, who are also largely responsible for the current pandemic and much more, are working relentlessly to ensure that the outcome will be an even harsher version of the system they have constructed for their own benefit."[7]

Naomi Klein, one of the most insightful ethical critics of corporate globalisation and capitalism, in her book *The Shock Doctrine: The Rise of Disaster Capitalism* (2007), has realistically proved how the neoliberal free market takes advantage of national crises or disasters ('shocks')—be they economic, political, military or natural—and the ensuing widespread desire to correct the situation. "They're not doing this because they think it's the most effective way to alleviate suffering during a pandemic—they have these ideas lying around that they now see an opportunity to implement."[8]

Against this larger historical and economic context, Klein categorically argues, "Coronavirus is the Perfect Disaster for Disaster Capitalism." Klein says we are already seeing "disaster capitalism" play out in the US. In response to the novel coronavirus, President Trump proposed a $700 billion stimulus package to bolster a battered economy. This would include cuts to payroll taxes which would devastate Medicare and social security. Moreover, it would not benefit people who have lost their jobs as small businesses have shut down.

Klein refers to 'America's crisis daddy' Andrew Cumo. His response to the post-COVID reality shows how large technological companies are going to profit from the pandemic. Google CEO Eric Schmidt will be heading a panel to reimagine New York state's potential to permanently integrate technology into every aspect of civic life. "The first priorities of what we're trying to do," Schmidt said, "are focused on telehealth, remote learning, and broadband…. We need to look for solutions that can be presented now, and accelerated, and use technology to make things better." Just a day earlier, Cuomo had announced a similar partnership with the Bill and Melinda Gates Foundation to develop "a smarter education system." Tech giants suggest "human-less, contactless technology" to curb pandemics. Anuja Sonalker, the CEO of Steer Tech, said, "Humans are biohazards, machines are not."[9]

While some are being brought to their knees, as in any crisis, others stand to win from the pandemic. Tech giants are joining forces on surveillance and supercomputing as nations scramble to get to grips with the technology. Amazon, Google, IBM and Microsoft have joined the COVID-19 High Performance Computing (HPC) consortium spearheaded by the White House Office of Science and Technology Policy, the US Department of Energy. Together, members will provide bioinformatics, epidemiology and molecular biology researchers with computing power to execute computational research on COVID-19. Facebook and Amazon have each participated in equity rounds since the WHO declared COVID-19 to be a pandemic in March 2020, and both are focusing on their investments in India. In April, Facebook invested $5.7 billion for a 10 per cent stake in India's largest telecom operator, Reliance Jio. Automakers have allied with med-tech companies to boost development of and access to COVID tests, vaccines, treatments and critical medical equipment. General Electric and Ford Motor will produce 50,000 ventilators for the US government under the Defence Production Act for $336 million. Ford Motor, the iconic American auto maker, is getting into the healthcare business in a big way, partnering with 3M, Thermo Fisher

Scientific and others to make respirators, face shields, gowns, ventilators and COVID-19 test kits.

As we have seen above, the savage beneficiaries of capitalism have already begun to cash in on the situation created by the pandemic. In Klein's view, pandemics/epidemics/disasters ('shocks') provide the "perfect condition" for governments and the global elite to implement unscrupulous policies (the "shock doctrine") and political and economic agendas by manipulating and aggravating existing inequalities ("shock therapy"), which would under 'normal' situations be met with great opposition and scrutiny, and profit from disasters ("disaster capitalism"). Klein refers to Milton Friedman to explain the "core tactical nostrum" of contemporary capitalism: "Only a crisis—actual or perceived—produces real change. When that crisis occurs, the actions that are taken depend on the ideas that are lying around. That, I believe, is our basic function: to develop alternatives to existing policies, to keep them alive and available until the politically impossible becomes politically inevitable."[10] Says Klein: "I call these orchestrated raids on the public sphere in the wake of catastrophic events, combined with the treatment of disasters as exciting market opportunities, 'disaster capitalism.'"[11] Klein provides the trajectory and genealogy of how global capitalists have historically profited from disasters.

In the second part of the book *The Shock Doctrine*, Klein discusses how Friedman used the "shock doctrine" effectively and comprehensively in the aftermath of the 1973 Chilean coup d'état ending Salvador Allende's presidency. It followed an extended period of sociopolitical unrest in the wake of US President Richard Nixon waging an economic warfare on Chile. Nixon had ordered the CIA to "make the economy scream" in Chile because he did not want Allende to push Chile into socialism and lose all US investments there. Allende's trusted chief Augusto Pinochet eventually assumed power in 1974.

The US promptly recognised the *junta* government and supported it in consolidating power. Milton and his Chicago Boys advised the dictator General Augusto Pinochet to make use of the political uncertainty to implement capitalist freedom. Pinochet and his Chicago Boys did their best to dismantle Chile's public sphere, auctioning off state enterprises and slashing financial and trade regulations. Enormous wealth was created in this period but at a terrible cost. By the early 1980s, Pinochet's Friedman-prescribed policies had caused rapid de-industrialisation, a tenfold increase in unemployment and an explosion of distinctly unstable shanty towns. They also led to a crisis of corruption and debt so severe that, in 1982, Pinochet was forced to fire his key Chicago Boy advisers and nationalise several of the large deregulated financial institutions.[12]

We can also find examples of how the "shock doctrine" was applied in South American economies in the 1970s, Poland, Russia, South Africa and the 'tiger economies'—originally used for Singapore, Taiwan, South Korea and Hong Kong—during the 1997 financial crisis. The use of "shock and awe" (technically known as rapid dominance) during the 2003 invasion of Iraq, which was "sold to the public on the basis of fear of weapons of mass destruction,"[13] is perhaps the most complete execution of the "shock doctrine" ever attempted; "history is a chronicle of shocks and aftermath."

Klein divulges the paradoxes of disaster capitalism:

Paul Bremer, appointed by [George] Bush to serve as director of the occupation authority in Iraq, admits that when he first arrived in Baghdad... "Baghdad was on fire, literally, as I drove in from the airport.... There was no traffic on the streets; there was no electricity anywhere; no oil production; no economic activity; there wasn't a single policeman on duty anywhere." And yet his solution to this crisis was to immediately fling open the country's borders to absolutely unrestricted imports: no tariffs, no duties, no inspections, no taxes. Iraq, Bremer declared two weeks after he arrived, was "open for business." Overnight, Iraq went from being one of the most isolated countries in the world, sealed off from the most basic trade by strict UN sanctions, to becoming the widest-open market anywhere. While the pickup trucks stuffed with loot were still being driven to buyers in Jordan, Syria and Iran, passing them in the opposite direction were convoys of flatbeds piled high with Chinese TVs, Hollywood DVDs and Jordanian satellite dishes, ready to be unloaded on the sidewalks of Baghdad's Karada district. Just as one culture was being burned and stripped for parts, another was pouring in, prepackaged, to replace it.... "One well-stocked 7-Eleven could knock out 30 Iraqi stores; a Wal-Mart could take over the country." Like the prisoners in Guantánamo's love shack, all of Iraq was going to be bought off with Pringles and pop culture—that, at least, was the Bush administration's idea of a postwar plan.[14]

As with the natural and human-induced disasters in the past, the political and economic elite know that COVID-19 is the 'perfect time' to push through their unpopular policies, plunder the resources for survival and further polarise nations and continents. The disaster capitalists and pro free-market corporations would even see the present crisis not only as a 'crisis of perception' but also a 'shock' to be resolved through abysmal economic policies. This would be implemented by 'maximising confusion' and 'minimising protection' to bail out global companies. If we follow our big media, we get the impression that it is not the death of the poor that we should worry about but the fact that markets are panicking, which Žižek defines as "capitalist animism."[15] Consequently, such capitalist animists prevent the coronavirus pandemic from evolving into organic moments where radically emancipatory and liberative policies emerge. This is the larger economic/material context in which we are called to make ekklēsia and diakonia happen by re/mapping the route of our collective future, including the logic of privatisation, as a panacea.

The current economic holocaust compels us to question the myth of capitalism and challenge its pretension as the saviour from the coronavirus pandemic. Boff rightly argues: "What will save us now are not private companies but the State with its public health policies—always under the attack of the free market system—and also the virtues of the new paradigm, advanced by many and also by me: care, social solidarity, co-responsibility and compassion."[16] We already see some positive shifts across the globe. The French President Emmanuel Macron, seemingly a neoliberal, was perhaps the first to express the resolve for such a change. While elaborating his schemes relating to protection of incomes and health outlays, he repeated three times *"quoi qu'il en coute"* ("whatever it costs"). It shows Macron's is not a panicky reaction but a strong commitment to pursue counter-cyclical policies and thus establish a Keynesian welfare state. He said:[17]

> My dear compatriots, tomorrow we shall have to learn the lessons of the time we're living through, question the development model our world has adopted for decades—whose failings are being exposed for all to see—and question the weaknesses of our democracies. What this pandemic is already revealing is that free healthcare not conditional on people's income, history or profession, and our welfare state, are not costs or burdens but precious assets, essential strengths when destiny strikes. What this pandemic is revealing is that there are goods and services that must be placed outside the laws of the market.

Recouping from COVID-19 could be at an appalling price. Neoliberals and capitalists will find the disaster a perfect opening for more all-pervading capitalism. As we have elucidated in this chapter, disaster capitalism is indeed forthright: it pronounces how the global elitist forces spring up to directly profit from large-scale disasters and wars. "It is only good for the rich; for the rest it is purgatory or hell and for nature it is relentless war."[18] Political forces exploit the crisis to push through unpopular deregulatory policies and a development agenda in the form of economic austerity, which systematically deepens the already worse inequality. In moments of crisis, naturally, people, especially the poor and the marginalised, trust governments for daily sustenance and survival. This is exactly where politics, economy and social structure perilously intersect. In as much as it worsens the existing economic plague, it also discloses that our interconnectedness is more than what our ruthless fiscal schemes would have us believe. It is in this intersecting space that ekklēsia and diakonia must happen.

COVID-19, Conspiracy Theory and Capitalism

COVID-19 appeared seemingly out of nowhere. As such, many have valid questions about the deadliness of the disease, its rapid spread and origin. Many are also speculating about the reasons behind the woeful response from governments across the world. Given the confusion, anger and mistrust, it is not surprising that certain theories—apparently providing an explanation that differ from the scientific consensus—have gained traction. One such pernicious conspiracy theory is that this virus is a bioweapon engineered by the Chinese state. These conspiracy theories distract us from the real source of all our problems—the capitalist system. In some cases, the divisive nature of conspiracy theories is even helpful for the ruling class, which is not averse to employing hysteria to its advantage. By manufacturing stories and events, rulers are able to divert attention from their own criminal actions, find scapegoats and place the blame on anyone or anything but themselves.

Not so surprisingly, capitalist forces favouring the Trump administration have taken advantage of the political posturing between US and China. Amid the Chinese virus rhetoric, the US threatened a trade war to force an exodus of manufacturers from China. Owing to mounting pressure, major companies supporting the US lobby are relocating from China to other South Asian nations. Indonesia is clearing up 4,000 hectares of land in Central Java to accommodate US companies planning to relocate from China in the wake of the pandemic and an escalating trade war. US lighting company Alpan plans to shift its production from Xiamen to Central Java in Indonesia to get around higher tariffs. US tech giant Apple began producing 3-4 million units—or about 30 per cent for the quarter—of its AirPod earphones in Vietnam in April 2020, a sign that the firm is relocating some of its supply chains away from China. Apple's suppliers, including Foxconn and Pegatron, and iPad maker Compal Electronics are also expanding operations in Vietnam. Inventec, an AirPods assembler, is reportedly building a plant in Vietnam.

With COVID-19 infecting millions across the world, China is facing an unprecedented global backlash that could destabilise its reign as the world's factory of choice. India is seeking to lure US businesses, including medical devices giant Abbott Laboratories, to relocate from China as Trump's administration steps up efforts to blame Beijing for its role in the pandemic. The government in April 2020 reached out to more than 1,000 companies in the US and through overseas missions to offer incentives for manufacturers seeking to move out of China. India is prioritising medical equipment suppliers, food processing units, textiles, leather and auto parts. As many as 100 US companies keen on exiting China are seriously considering Uttar Pradesh as their new destination. The diplomatic and military stand-off between China and India also provide a perfect storm for US companies to profit from the trade war and conspiracy theories. It could even be 'conspiracy capitalism'; capitalism thrives on geopolitical and racial conspiracies.

Capitalism and the 'Pandemic of Caste'

The coronavirus pandemic is a public health crisis that is capitalism's collateral damage. In every crisis, what resurfaces in India is caste. Influential Dalit thinker Chandra Bhan Prasad believed that "capitalism would break the caste system" and will "turn caste order into a relic." Capitalism as an economic system is expected to usher in a market rationality through which the role of social identities gradually becomes insignificant. The market-oriented economy and the investment and growth that it has spurred have finally created a pathway to 'progress' for many Dalits. Migration to cities is one key aspect of this process.

According to Dalit Indian Chamber of Commerce & Industry (DCCCI) founder chairman Milind Kamble, "caste and capitalism can't co-exist." Caste and localism are inseparable; that is why the caste system is able to thrive in villages. In local set-ups, members of the society know each other's caste and the so-called upper caste exercises its superiority over the lower caste. In a city, people do not know each other and, therefore, anonymity comes into force and the caste order loses its grip. Moreover, the core value system in capitalism is profit. In order to make profit, the system becomes blind to caste. Capitalism has also introduced many caste-neutral occupations. For instance, repairing computers or mobiles has no caste identity. Cleaning staff in hotels, malls and corporate offices are becoming caste neutral. By introducing mechanised cleaning kits and by giving uniforms to workers, the job of a house cleaner has gained respectability.

But COVID-19 and the disastrous lockdown have proved that wealth does have caste (while poverty does not). Capitalism and migration did not eradicate the untouchable ghettos. Dalits migrated to cities to pull rickshaws, to construction sites, to carry loads and for sanitation work. The upper class moved to cities for education, business and white-collar employment. The modern idea of work/labour was only a myth. As in the villages, caste is premised on untouchability, restrictions and disciplining bodies. As the lockdown made it clear, India is one nation of two worlds: the ruling 'upper caste-class' world and 'working caste-class' world. Notwithstanding its virtuous goal, the lockdown denied Dalits access to food, water, shelter, medicines and jobs. The transmission of coronavirus has clearly been caste-class based.

More than the virus, the massive reverse exodus of migrant workers to their respective villages, the lockdown and the government's response to COVID made them more vulnerable to illness and death. The capitalist jingle of "the well-being of all" in a caste-ridden society is only a manifestation of the kind of *savarna* disdain that characterises the current social caste-scape of COVID 'Brahminism'. In the current coronavirus pandemic, only a Dalit 'biopolitical power' that holds the state responsible can protect human life and ensure economic freedom as opposed to the neoliberal regimes that minimise state intervention in the circulation and growth of capital.[19]

Covenantal Desires, Manna Economy and Materiality of Faith

Responding to the pandemic-induced havoc as a faith community is what ekklēsia and diakonia means now. Faith cannot remain ethically innocent to the corporatist crusades in the age of COVID, which is, as Rabbi Jonathan Sacks qualifies, "the nearest we have to a revelation for atheists." Nor can faith be an apolitical fantasy of rapture or an ethereal escape from the world focused on saving souls. Economic justice is a deep faith issue as it matters to God. The Manna economy in the book of Exodus testifies to the fact that God is interested in, and hence intervenes in, the material needs of his people.

The deliverance of the people of Israel from Egypt was an exodus from the regime of unwarranted coveting. For common sense reasons the liberated slaves wanted to go back to Pharaoh's economy of desire system that had made them mere biological bodies (Ex 16:2-3). They were unsure of an alternative desire and economy as they were conditioned by Pharaoh's 'usurpatious' system of monopolising all forms of food production and distribution. In Exodus 16, God exposed them to risk and scarcity. Wilderness is exterior to the sphere of Pharaoh's control of commodities and "slices of avaricious desire." God provided them the gift of meat (16:13), bread (16:14) and water (17:1–7). Life is sustained not through coveting, but though sharing of life resources and practising divine generosity. The Manna economy strongly denounces and refuses the capitalist logic of profit, economy of extraction and commodity acquisition. For the faith community, it is an alternative model to the capitalist model of sustenance of life, which is pushed by anxiety about scarcity.

Jesus' initial pronouncement as recorded in Luke 4:18-19 is an indication of the material (this-worldly or pro-life) accent of his earthly mission. Jesus' ministry was always in defiance of the exploitative economy and imperial hegemony of the Roman Empire. Joerg Rieger writes, "Of the 31 parables in the Synoptic Gospels, more than half (19) reflect directly on class, inequality, worker pay, indebtedness, the misuse of wealth, and the distribution of wealth."[20] This is further intensified in the last judgement narratives in Matthew's Gospel (Matt 25:31-46). Contrary to the economic virus in the form of patronage system, privatism and otherworldly (non-material) spirituality in his time, Jesus suggested alternative economics (Kingdom of God economics) of radical participatory sharing, not percolatory prosperity. Participatory sharing envisions "participatory socialism" (Thomas Piketty). It has the inexorable potential for conflict with capitalist norms and practices. If participatory sharing is diakonia, then it makes happen an ekklēsia that is participatory and socialist in being and doing.

This calls for reimagining lockdown weariness as a sabbath rest for all creation (cf. Ps 31).[21] Like the people of Israel in the brickyards of Pharaoh, the privilege of sabbath rest is not affordable for migrant labourers and daily wage workers. Therefore, sabbath rest means allowing everyone's lifeworld to function without stressing anyone. Those who do not respect the anxiety of the working class of contracting the coronavirus live in 'Promethean time'—time is money and profit.[22] For such people with a 'Promethean agenda' —President Trump for instance—quarantine is frustrating and fatiguing as they cannot accomplish, achieve and possess something to the extent they want to. This is contrary to the "covenantal time," as Brueggemann calls it, which is marked by freedom, compassion, justice and fidelity. Hence, diakonia in the current context means responding to the pandemic through the lens of covenantal time, which ensures sabbath rest to all around us. It implies the earth getting sabbath from pollution, roads getting sabbath from accidents, etc. If diakonia means practising covenantal time, the ekklēsia thus evolves is a covenantal ekklēsia.

It is important for a faith community that is committed to economic and political justice to unpack the cryptic paraenesis of Romans 13:1-7 in order to fashion a disposition towards the state and the universality of global capital. In Paul's explication of civic authority, we find both its theological justification and hidden ideological content (Rom 13:4). He criticises the infallibility of the ideological and violent apparatuses of the state by saying "all authority is from God." Global capital is the new emperor. In an age of capital, Romans 13:1–7 provides enough clues to the faith community to become aware of the theological justifications the conservatives often furnish to endorse the rhetoric of capitalism, such as progress, development and modernism. The lack of alternatives in Romans 13 (continue to pay taxes) reminds us of the totalising effect of the political-financial capitalist ideology. A new political subjectivity formed by a deep solidarity with those on the margins could be a viable alternative to the politics of caste and capital.

Conclusion

The alternative economics of radical participatory sharing is rooted in counter-desires for cooperation and interdependence. This is the basis for mature materiality of faith and praxis. Materiality of faith is not to be confused with materialism. For Brueggemann, materiality is central to the Christian faith on two fronts: God created the world and found good, affirming the essential goodness of all creation; and, Jesus assumed matter/flesh/body to save the material world.[23] Thus matter and material reality become the locus and beneficiary of Jesus' saving activity. In the life of the early church too, we find the practice of a shared economy where materiality is an important aspect of witnessing. It is in practising (diakonia) such a 'gospel-imagination' that ekklēsia becomes a shared space and a participatory fellowship.

Endnotes

[1] https://www.imf.org/en/News/Articles/2020/04/07/sp040920-SMs2020-Curtain-Raiser (9 April 2020)

[2] Dominic Rushe (13 August 2020). https://www.theguardian.com/business/2020/aug/13/us-unemployment-latest-figures-coronavirus-claims

[3] https://www.thehindu.com/business/Economy/us-crude-futures-turn-negative-for-first-time-on-scant-storage-weak-demand/article31392254.ece (21 April 2020)

[4] Interview with Noam Chomsky, by Jipson John and Jithesh P. M. https://thewire.in/world/noam-chomsky-interview-covid-19-pandemic-capitalism-neoliberalism-us-hegemony.

[5] Colin Todhunter, "Coronavirus Capitalism: Entrenching Dispossession and Dependency," 21 April 2020).

https://countercurrents.org/2020/04/coronavirus-capitalism-entrenching-dispossession-and-dependency/

[6] Josh Zumbrun *and* David Harrison, "IMF, World Bank Face Deluge of Aid Requests from Developing World," 9 April 2020). https://www.wsj.com/articles/imf-world-bank-face-deluge-of-aid-requests-from-developing-world-11586424609

[7] Interview with Noam Chomsky, by Jipson John and Jithesh P. M. https://thewire.in/world/noam-chomsky-interview-covid-19-pandemic-capitalism-neoliberalism-us-hegemony.

[8] Marie Solis, "Coronavirus Is the Perfect Disaster for Disaster Capitalism," (14 March 2020). https://readersupportednews.org/opinion2/277-75/61852-focus-naomi-klein-coronavirus-is-the-perfect-disaster-for-disaster-capitalism?fbclid=IwAR1VpzlwyScbWEcv57JYD7fBonM-gzPUfnJx-d8MzCZuC32qoucg2ei3k6oM

[9] Naomi Klein, "How big tech plans to profit from the pandemic," (13 May 2020). https://www.theguardian.com/news/2020/may/13/naomi-klein-how-big-tech-plans-to-profit-from-coronavirus-pandemic?fbclid=IwAR1z

LUzv611yxtLphPDZ6DsZaOSRHzlfJgHAaesQuoBVNX19PyhoxbkwNO8

[10] Milton Friedman, *Capitalism and Freedom* (Chicago: The University of Chicago, 2002), ix.

[11] Naomi Klein, *The Shock Doctrine*, Penguin Books Ltd. Kindle Edition, 6.

[12] Naomi Klein, "Milton Friedman did not Save," (3 March 2020). https://www.theguardian.com/commentisfree/cifamerica/2010/mar/03/chile-earthquake

[13] Klein, Naomi. *The Shock Doctrine*, Penguin Books Ltd. Kindle Edition, 327.

[14] Klein, Naomi. *The Shock Doctrine*, Penguin Books Ltd. Kindle Edition, 339-340.

[15] Žižek, *Pandemic*, 44

[16] Mada Jurado (26 March 2020). https://novenanews.com/theologian-coronavirus-different-relationship-earth/?fbclid=IwAR0icJ-fyG3TZYF6MNP_Sym_F6BXZPnXkB2oMUfnxh31SFmNW2WQj4p1IXM

[17] https://franceintheus.org/spip.php?article9654 (16 March 2020)

[18] Cameron Doody (2 May 2020). https://novenanews.com/liberation-theologian-boff-capitalism-nature-war/?fbclid=IwAR3APtmB_C1tnRrx5PBqEgSBpHhHQWct5FGmPCPeyzSoGTqNq213Rfdhbe0

[19] Adarsh Priyadarshi, "Biopower and the spectre of capital," (21 June 2020). https://medium.com/@2adarshpriyadarshi/biopower-and-the-spectre-of-capital-a49f7545f2b5

[20] Joerg Rieger, "Why Economic Justice Mattes to God," (19 June 2020). https://www.religionandjustice.org/blog/why-economic-justice-matters-to-god

[21] Walter Brueggemann, "Quarantine Fatigue or Sabbath Rest," (7 May 2020). https://churchanew.org/brueggemann/2020/05/07/brueggemann3?rq=Sabbath

[22] Walter Brueggemann, "Quarantine Fatigue or Sabbath Rest," (7 May 2020). https://churchanew.org/brueggemann/2020/05/07/brueggemann3?rq=Sabbath

[23] Walter Brueggemann. *Materiality as Resistance* (Kentucky: John Knox Press, 2020), Kindle Location, 14

Chapter 3

Democracy and Digital Imperialism

The tradition of the oppressed teaches us that the 'state of emergency'
in which we live is the not exception but the rule.

Walter Benjamin

(...) in order to see perfect disciplines functioning, rulers dreamt
of the state of plague.

Michel Foucault

Introduction

The UN Human Rights Office identified a dozen Asia-Pacific countries that sought to deprive people of their right to freedom of expression during the COVID-19 crisis: Bangladesh, Cambodia, China, India, Indonesia, Malaysia, Myanmar, Nepal, the Philippines, Sri Lanka, Thailand and Vietnam. Expressing alarm at this clampdown on freedom of expression, the UN High Commissioner for Human Rights, Michelle Bachelet, in a statement on 3 June 2020, said that emergency powers should not be weaponised by governments to

> ...quash dissent, control the population, and even perpetuate their time in power. They should be used to cope effectively with

the pandemic—nothing more, nothing less. Shooting, detaining, or abusing someone for breaking a curfew because they are desperately searching for food is clearly an unacceptable and unlawful response.[1]

India's faltering democracy index hurt its battle against COVID. Amid India's lockdown to check the spread of COVID, the police cleared Shaheen Bagh in capital Delhi of those who had been protesting against the Citizenship (Amendment) Act, or CAA, for over 100 days. The protest sites at Nizamuddin, Turkman Gate and Seelampur in Delhi too were also cleared.

In this quest to exercise authority for "the greater good," the government also employed a grim tool—the calculated suppression of dissent. For instance, Safoora Zargar, the 27-year-old student of Jamia Milia Islamia, who was active in the anti-CAA protests, was arrested in April under the Unlawful Activities (Prevention) Act, or the UAPA, which was originally passed in the wake of rising terrorist activity and violent contentions in the country. Zargar, lodged in an overcrowded jail at Tihar, was denied bail until late June despite the numerous health risks because of a complicated pregnancy. Even doctors were not immune from suppression during a pandemic. Indranil Khan, who spoke about the lack of adequate personal protective equipment (PPE) in Kolkata hospitals, was charged under the Indian Penal Code with "causing disharmony and a feeling of hatred that disturbed public tranquillity." Later, Devangana Kalita and Natasha Narwal, student activists of the feminist advocacy collective Pinjra Tod, were arrested from their homes on charges of "obstructing public servants in discharge of public functions through force." Narwal was booked under the UAPA.

India, however, cannot be singled out in this regard. Thailand's Prime Minister Gen Prayut Chan-o-cha barred journalists from directly reporting on the pandemic through medical professionals; Hungary's Prime Minister Viktor Orbán declared an indefinite state of emergency allowing him to "rule by decree" with powers of censorship; and Israeli Prime Minister Benjamin Nethanyu suspended courts while he faced charges of corruption—a move that was met with the first "socially distant protests" in April 2020.

However, the world was not bereft of displays of public defiance either. In the US, the death of African American George Floyd at the hands of a white police officer, Derek Chauvin, sparked fervent protests across the country. The incident acted as a major tipping point for a community that has endured entrenched brutality for centuries. Health risks of COVID did not prevent them from taking to the streets as the situation warranted mass protests.

Biopolitical Technocracy and Pandemic Rhetoric of War

Simukai Chigudu, a Zimbabwean political scientist who documented the cholera outbreak in Zimbabwe in 2008, has noted that "every phase of an epidemic [pandemic too]—origins, pattern of unfolding, who lives and who dies, response and rehabilitation, aftermath in civic life—is largely a social calculus." The epidemiological and political responses to COVID-19 have revealed relationships between disease, technocracy and governmental accountability. Authoritarian and totalitarian governments will and have used the pandemic to consolidate power, curb individual liberties and restrict the space for civil society organisations and freedom of expression. Democratic and authoritarian societies alike are ramping up surveillance of their citizens as part of their attempts to stop the spread of the virus. The pandemic has been marked less by medical achievements and more by the arrests of politically active youth involved in expressing disapproval of government policies.

We were cautioned, right from the first wave of COVID, by whistleblowers and organic intellectuals that authoritarian governments would naturally use the 'frozen in time' situation as an opportunity to regimentalise and militarise the systems of governance. American whistleblower Edward Snowden categorically warned us that autocratic governments would definitely try to build "the architecture of oppression."[2] Even in democratic countries like the US, as Yale historian Timothy Snyder opined, "it is pretty much inevitable" that a president in the person of "Trump will try to stage a coup and overthrow democracy because of the unprecedented verging of theocratic, aristocratic and authoritarian oligarchy."[3] Whether Snyder's prediction of a potential coup in the US becomes a reality or not, we can already see instances of the state of emergency made normal and regular in the name of preventing the 'pathogen intruder' (coronavirus).

President Trump has been at loggerheads with the state governments since the spread of the coronavirus in the US. He used the pandemic as an excuse to exert his authority over the states and supersede governors and override their decisions. He challenged state-issued stay-at-home orders aimed at controlling the pandemic. Trump took the same monocratic approach in the issue of opening churches for worship: "I call upon governors nationwide to allow our churches and places of worship to open right now. If they don't do it, I will override the governors."

From Russia, the Philippines, Ghana, Hungary, Israel and India we hear awful stories of leaders imposing punitive surveillance laws and biopolitical disciplinary projects to make the people of the state "docile biomass." The Russian government introduced CCTVs with facial recognition software (techno-totalitarianism), mobile apps that can access user location to track potential virus carriers, mobile phone data, QR codes and credit card records to contain mass infection. But these extremely intrusive and aggressive electronic measures that surpass basic controlled surveillance are apparently laying the foundation for a "cybergulag." Philippines President Rodrigo Duterte warned protesters who attempted to violate his "enhanced community quarantine" laws that he would order police and military personnel to shoot them down. Israel's Prime Minister Benjamin Netanyahu authorised the Shin Bet internal security service to tap a previously undisclosed trove of mobile phone data, customarily used for anti-terrorism activities, circumventing parliamentary scrutiny, to trace the movements of infected people. Netanyahu's caretaker government also suspended all courts and legal entities and imposed a six-month prison sentence for anyone, except visitors and lawyers, who breached lockdown regulations. India's COVID-19 contact-tracing (health surveillance) app, Aarogya Setu—which means 'bridge to health' in Sanskrit—has faced allegations of invasion of privacy and poor security.

Most countries, especially Russia, China and Israel, have used biometric surveillance technology to curb the pandemic. Fifty years ago, the KGB, the Soviet Union's security agency, relied on flesh-and-blood spooks to observe the Russian people. Benjamin Netanyahu sanctioned the country's security agency to deploy omnipresent radars and sophisticated algorithms, customarily held in reserve for fighting terrorists, to locate coronavirus patients. To bypass the rebuttal from the parliamentary subcommittee, Netanyahu rammed it through with an "emergency pudding decree." The most notable case, though, is China. It started monitoring people's smartphones, use facial recognition cameras and mobile apps to warn people about their proximity to infected patients.

By using the political rhetoric of war, as Trump who defines himself as a "wartime president" did, the state and the government manipulate the collective panic and paranoia to militarise the pandemic. People naturally prioritise health over privacy. And the state plays the role of a caregiver to save people from the paralysing medical uncertainty that ensue disasters. This would enable authoritarian governments to deploy apparently innocuous mass surveillance through disciplinary tactics and strict spatial distancing: "exceptional circumstances breed exceptional measures." The state-sponsored draconian surveillance, under the pretext of combating the coronavirus, can become a biopolitical project that dismantles democratic rights and privacy, making citizens, as the state fantasises, to become tamed bio-civilians. This is the breeding ground for a disciplined populace and the reinforcing of state agenda; "pandemic is provisional, statism steamrolls."[4]

Any effort to map out the archaeology of how various governments responded to pandemics will point to the birth of a "disciplined majority." This is accomplished largely through intimidating technological interventions and spatial segregation.[5] Deploying of coercive surveillance to pathologically intrude into the life of the people to facilitate disciplining and to underpin the viral ideology of those in authority is not new. Michel Foucault, in his book *Discipline and Punish: The Birth of the Prison*, records this shift in attitude towards punishment from public spectacle (torture) to private detention and surveillance (prison): "If it is true that the leper gave rise to rituals of exclusion, which to a certain extent provided the model for, and general form of the great Confinement, then the plague gave rise to disciplinary projects."[6] Disciplining measures strengthen both state power and governments' xenophobic grip over *demos*.

Organic intellectuals and various progressive social movements believe that undemocratic forces might blatantly use the surveillance during the pandemic to consolidate their political power by sneakily defeating democracy. Interim emergency measures could very likely become a fixture in life. Israeli public intellectual and historian Yuval Noah Harari observes, "The epidemic might nevertheless mark an important watershed in the history of surveillance." [7] Harari gives two examples. First, the state of emergency declared in Israel during the 1948 War of Independence, which justified a range of harsh measures such as press censorship and land confiscation to special regulations for making pudding, continued till 2011. Second, nineteenth century scientists have discovered that hand washing is important for personal hygiene. Now billions of people wash their hands, not because they are scared of the "soap police," but rather because they understand scientific facts and health guidelines.

The outrageous decision by New York Governor Andrew Cuomo to cancel the June democratic presidential primary on health grounds was the one of the moves to silence the progressives in the state. We see similar attempts in the subcontinent, especially in India. For the people of India, the lockdown period was somewhat of an executive emergency. Under a colonial era act on disaster management, the government undermined judicial oversight, federal principles, cross-party discussions, procedural matters and core democratic principles. Any such "protective" moves to suspend public discourse might look justifiable, but the startling triumph of the narrative of the essential deferral of democratic events could become a model template for future autocrats when India resumes a semblance of normalcy. It is near certain that we need to live with the coronavirus as it is going stay with us for some time; so the expedient platitude of "we can think of well-being only if we live" with which we began the war against the virus could become a licence to minimise democracy, if not cut it to size forever.

The irony of this no-end-in-view situation is that the epidemic occurred at a time when pop-scientific media was obsessed with two aspects of the digitalisation of our lives. On the one hand, a lot is being written about the new phase of capitalism, called "surveillance capitalism"—a digital control over our lives exerted by state agencies and private corporations. On the other hand is the topic of direct brain-machine interface ('wired brain'). When our brain is connected to digital machines, we can cause things to happen in reality just by thinking about them. Then, my brain is directly connected to another brain so that another individual can directly share my experience. Extrapolated to its extreme, wired brain opens up the prospect of "the restless genius" and "the ultimate thinking machine." Ray Kurzweil, one of the world's leading thinker and futurist, called "the technological singularity" (simply, the singularity) the divine-like space of shared global awareness. It is a hypothetical point in time at which advancement of artificial intelligence and other technologies become unrestrained and irreversible, resulting in unforeseeable and irremediable changes to human civilisation. Whatever the scientific status of this idea—dubious, for the time being—it is clear that its realisation will affect the basic features of humans as thinking/speaking beings.

Epidemic Singularity

The eventual rise of the singularity will be apocalyptic in the complex meaning of the term—it implies the encounter with a truth hidden in our ordinary human existence, i.e. the entry into a new post-human dimension. It is interesting to note that the extensive use of surveillance was quietly accepted—drones were used not only in China, but also in Italy and Spain. As for the spiritual vision of the singularity, the new direct unity of the human and the divine, a bliss in which we leave behind the limits of our corporeal existence, can well turn out to be a new unimaginable nightmare. From a critical standpoint, it would be difficult to decide which is worse (a greater threat to humanity): the viral devastation of our lives or the loss of our individuality in the singularity. Epidemics remind us that we remain firmly rooted in bodily existence with all the dangers that this implies.

According to Giorgio Agamben,[8] states use the narrative of the pandemic as a war-like situation to militarise democratic institutions. People think authoritarianism is the best option in the time of pandemic and war. This they achieve through frantic and irrational emergency measures with severe limitation on human mobility; "the securitization of public space, self-isolation and 'lockdowns' constitute a challenge to the norms of democratic politics and everyday life."[9] In Žižek's view, Agamben's reaction is the extreme form of a widespread leftist stance of reading the "exaggerated panic" caused by the virus as a mixture of an exercise of social control combined with elements of outright racism. However, the measures necessitated by the epidemics should not be automatically reduced to the usual paradigm of surveillance and control propagated by thinkers like Foucault.[10]

One might agree with Agamben's remark that "the containment measures against COVID are being used as an 'exception' to allow an extraordinary expansion of the governmental powers of imposing extraordinary restrictions on our freedoms."[11] Governments have regularised the 'exceptions' in exceptional situations, which they eventually perceive as a "non-choice" ("non-exceptionality of exceptions"), thus regulating all human discourses and social relations. It is true that exceptions become 'normal' in a world of "technical interconnections" because "viral" itself is political, social, medical and technological, says the French philosopher Jean-Luc Nancy.[12] But you cannot use the same argument to justify the suspension of democratic rights.

Our hitherto exclusively natural human experiences are now the locus of innovative interventions of biotechnology. Consequently, our biological life and political discourses have "progressively formed an ever tighter knot, with problematic and sometimes tragic results." This naturally leads to a process of "medicalisation of politics" and a "politicisation of medicine." While the former focuses on "curing" and is unburdened by ideological commitment, the arbitrary task of the latter is social control. This explains the enormously diverse valuations virologists are making on the mutations and the intensity of the pandemic. It is a fascist logic because biopolitics see people as "segments of population differentiated according to health, age, gender or even ethnic group" and not as individuals or communities.

Put differently, society believes in and seeks to protect only "naked life." For Agamben, "bare life" corresponds to the ancient Greek term *zoe*, which expresses the simple fact of living— "Bare life is life which can be killed but not yet sacrificed."[13] This differs from the term *bios,* which denotes a qualified life—a life with dignity, endowed with meaning which is consequently considered "worthy" of sacrifice. In the classical world, *zoe* was excluded from the *polis* and confined to the sphere of the *oikos,* the home. This is the very place where social distancing measures and public health interventions by the state seek to confine us. We are repeatedly told to stay at home and wash our hands. Furthermore, the figure of "bare life" appears to be stripped of all agency and dignity.[14] Human life without dignity, freedom and democratic rights is just "naked life" or "biomass." The quarantining of democracy through a technocracy in the name of the pandemic thus becomes a catalyst for digital imperialism. This necessitates an initiative for alternative liberative vision to reclaim human dignity.

Perhaps technological upheaval is an inevitable consequence of our attempts to contain the pandemic. The immediate task of the governments would be to deal with the virus. They may not be concerned about how technological feudalism is going to transform how society is constituted. Amartya Sen contends that overcoming a gigantic health crisis like COVID-19 is not like fighting a war where the top-down model of political governance works best. In contrast, Sen proposes, "What is needed for dealing with a social calamity is participatory governance and alert public discussion."[15]

COVID-19, Digital Dalit and Dalit Cyberspace

A 14-year-old Dalit girl, Devika, from Valanchery, Malappuram district, Kerala, reportedly set herself ablaze and died on 1 June 2020. Her parents, Balakrishnan and Sheeba, said their daughter was upset about not having access to a TV or online classes. They said Devika was a bright student and could not bear the disappointment of losing out on important Class IX classes.

"There is a television at home but that has not been working. She told me it needed to be repaired but I couldn't get it done. I couldn't afford a smartphone either," the girl's father, a daily wage worker with little income during the coronavirus lockdown, told reporters. The young girl's mother had given birth only a few weeks ago and the family had hardly any money.

Kuldip Kumar from Gummer village near Himachal Pradesh's Jawalamukhi town was in deep distress after his school decided to move lessons online. But Kumar did not have a mobile phone or the money to buy one. He tried to get a loan of Rs. 6,000 from banks and even private lenders but his efforts were in vain. Finally, he had to sell his cow. Kumar's plight received a lot of attention after the media highlighted it. Many came forward to help him.

However, there are many who have not been so lucky. Take, for instance, the primary school in the Kota Gunjapur village of Madhya Pradesh's Panna district. It has 31 registered students. After the school received orders to hold classes online, the principal, Rohni Pathak, organised a door-to-door survey to assess its feasibility. "We found that households of only eight of the 31 students had mobile phones and just two were active," Pathak said. Hakki Bai, a daily wage labourer belonging to the Gond tribal community, whose 13-year-old son Brij Kumar studies in the school, said the family did not have a phone. She said: "Even if we buy one, there is no power supply to charge it. I don't know how he will catch up with studies once the classes start." Pathak said the situation was the same in other villages. Education is just one area that has highlighted the digital divide between India's rural and urban areas during the lockdown. It was evident in other areas too like telemedicine, banking, e-commerce, e-governance, all of which were accessible only via internet during the lockdown.

India is among those countries whose educational institutions, including schools, have been shut down to slow the spread of COVID. Until September, these educational institutions had not set any date for reopening despite the growing concerns of various stakeholders over the prolonged lockdown's immediate, short-term and long-term impact on students, parents and society at large. It is in this context that an understanding of the impact of COVID on school education, with special focus on digitally-deprived children, gains importance. Free and compulsory education is a fundamental right as guaranteed by the Constitution, but India's school educational system has traditionally seen structural imbalances with respect to class, caste, language, region, development (urban and rural) and gender divides.

The move towards a universal online education and examination system affects marginalised caste groups in two specific ways. First, their access to the means of participation in online education is terribly low, especially in rural India. Second, the lockdown has unleashed a brutal livelihood crisis for the working class in rural India. The absolute loss in gainful employment for landless manual workers in India has hit Dalit and Adivasi families in the countryside the worst. Education thus becomes the first casualty for students from poor working class families. The responsibility of the faith community is to be in solidarity with the struggles of the marginalised and Dalit collectives for a "democratic opening" in the digital divide. It aims, as P. Thirumal and Gary Michael Tartakov rightly say:

To constitute a Cyberspace outside the realm of the Hindu cosmic order and the nation-state. Thus, for the Dalits, the Internet offers a terrain for exploitation of their community interests in social activism that is relatively casteless, nationally, and even internationally, extensive and so potentially useful in ways no previous medium has been before.[16]

Ekklēsia and Diakonia: Political Survivalism and Public Humanity

Ekklēsia and diakonia are incessantly evolving praxiological imaginations. They assume new forms of incarnations depending on the context and its challenges. In the context of the pandemic where technocracy and digital feudalism become a major threat to daily justice, ekklēsia happens through the diaconal practice of daily fights for democratic justice. Democracy is the best system we have in place thus far to ensure everyday justice; democracy is in a way a celebration of daily justice. Faith cannot remain on the political periphery when freedom to dissent is quarantined.[17] Quarantining dissent means quarantining democracy itself. People are not just biomass or data or sheep, but free persons created in the image of God. Freedom is the most important feature of the image of God. It allows human beings to participate in the social process without fear, which makes human beings accountable to historical situations and material realities.

While following enforced lockdown and quarantining protocol, the faith community is keen on apolitical survivalism. "Apolitical survivalism" not only brackets human sociality, but more importantly it makes human beings asocial. Being human means "being-in-relation" (community of inter-beings); we are beings in relationships (community of life). Relationality constitutes the very being of human. This is precisely what the southern African Ubuntu philosophy professes: "I am because we are"; Ubuntu is that nebulous concept of common humanity, oneness: humanity, both you and me.[18] This is different from the world of anthropoids. It compels human beings to be a participant in all forms of social relations and democratic phenomenon. Denying the ontological compulsions means denying human beings what makes them human. This explains why the faith community must address digital imperialism and technocracy.

The Tower of Babel is perhaps one of the earliest examples of humanity's insatiable desire to regulate the movements of human bodies (Gen 11:1–9). This constitutes a challenge to the divine command to "fill the earth" (Gen 1:28). They used technology (bricks and tar) to build an empire that would gain access to heaven for themselves as they were afraid of being scattered over the face of the earth (11:4). Did those who made the decision to build the tower represent the entire community? Whose interest did they serve by restricting the migration of people? What and who would have been on the losing end if people migrated? Who suggested the use of technology and "good intentions" as a means to regulate people's democratic rights? Did anyone oppose the decision to build the tower? The same questions pop up when we see the state using its apparatus to regimentalise people using digital technology.

The story fits well with Israelite descriptions of Babylon. Nimrod, who is explicitly credited with the building of Babel (Gen 10:8–12), is a mirror image of Nebuchadnezzar. In the book of Daniel, images of great height are used to depict and criticise the power and arrogance of Babylon (gigantic statue in Daniel 2; 60-cubit high gold image of the emperor in Daniel 3, and the great tree in Dan 4). The use of technology to control people and their movement is technological imperialism. God acts swiftly to reclaim people's freedom and their right to move. Governments using technology to control people and their democratic rights in the pretext of curbing COVID is against God's intention. As in the story of the Tower of Babel, state governments unilaterally exercise power over people to make a name for themselves, which they achieve by deprivileging the other.

Jethro, the priest of Midian, Moses' father-in-law, advised Moses to delegate the juridical responsibility of making decisions concerning people and settling their issues (Ex 18:17–24). In imperial regimes, judicial and political institutions/apparatuses are dysfunctional. State is sovereign. Moses was following the Egyptian logic of sovereignty, wherein the Pharaoh becomes the answer to all their problems. Perhaps Moses wanted to be sovereign in exceptional situations, as in the wilderness. But Jethro advises a new leadership structure. Exceptional situations must be used as an opportunity to establish democratic/covenantal institutions. Situations should not be used as an excuse to monopolise/centralise power. Jethro's criticism of Moses' Egyptian model of imperial leadership can help us problematise digital imperialism and how it weakens democracy.

Democracy is perhaps one of the most important mutually constituting premises for both ekklēsia and diakonia. Ekklēsia was the principal assembly of democracy in ancient Athens. The first-century Christian community named their gathering 'ekklēsia' to keep their fellowship as a political assemblage where people gather, discuss and debate on common issues. This is significant in the context of COVID, when governments have taken on undue authority to subvert people's freedom and democratic rights.

Conclusion

The coronavirus challenges us of our identity construction as "homo hierarchicus" or hierarchical humans. Any attempt to dehumanise people by political agencies must be challenged politically. Such a diaconal process would definitely require secularising creedal and doctrinal expressions of faith itself. This "prophetic politics"[19] that radically changes how we make sense of social realities means two things: politicisation of faith and materiality of faith. It calls us to collaborate with democratic initiatives and prophetic experiments such as the Occupy Wall Street and the Black Lives Matter movements in the US and protests that fight the lynching of Dalits in India. This is what "prophetic diakonia" means in the context of technocracy, which is achieved by focusing on the schism between prophetic voices and political institutions. In this process, ekklēsia becomes a true democratic social apostolate and an assemblage of public humanity.

<u>Excerpts from Advocate Prasanth Bhushan's Statement
to the Supreme Court</u>

[Prashant Bhushan read out the following statement in the Supreme Court on 20 August 2020, during the hearing conducted by the court to decide his penalty after they found him guilty of contempt for his tweets on Chief Justice of India S.A. Bobde and the Supreme Court.]

"I find it hard to believe that the Court finds my tweet 'has the effect of destabilizing the very foundation of this important pillar of Indian democracy'. I can only reiterate that these two tweets represented my bonafide beliefs, the expression of which must be permissible in any democracy. Indeed, public scrutiny is desirable for healthy functioning of judiciary itself.

I believe that open criticism of any institution is necessary in a democracy, to safeguard the constitutional order....Failing to speak up would have been a dereliction of duty, especially for an officer of the court like myself....It would be insincere and contemptuous on my part to offer an apology for the tweets that expressed what was and continues to be my bonafide belief.

I do not ask for mercy. I do not appeal to magnanimity. I am here, therefore, to cheerfully submit to any penalty that can lawfully be inflicted upon me for what the Court has determined to be an offence, and what appears to me to be the highest duty of a citizen."

Endnotes

1 https://www.ohchr.org/EN/NewsEvents/Pages/DisplayNews.aspx?NewsID=25828&LangID=E (27 April 2020).

2 Trone Dowd, "Snowden Warns Governments Are Using Coronavirus to Build 'the Architecture of Oppression,'" (13 April 2020). https://www.vice.com/en_in/article/bvge5q/snowden-warns-governments-are-using-coronavirus-to-build-the-architecture-of-oppression

3 Chauncey Devega (1 May 2017). https://www.salon.com/2017/05/01/historian-timothy-snyder-its-pretty-much-inevitable-that-trump-will-try-to-stage-a-coup-and-overthrow-democracy/?fbclid=IwAR3V304SQoaZm1US6YUaszjW1BRWKcDcDf2UHBCbjrp-6pOzv3-lv8FsNiM

4 Shamayita Sen and Debabrota Basu, "Catch-22 of a pandemic: Inception of a disciplined majority," (22 April 2020). https://armchairjournal.com/catch-22-of-a-pandemic-inception-of-a-disciplined-majority/

5 Shamayita Sen and Debabrota Basu, "Catch-22 of a pandemic: Inception of a disciplined majority," (22 April 2020). https://armchairjournal.com/catch-22-of-a-pandemic-inception-of-a-disciplined-majority/

6 Michel Foucault, *Discipline and Punish: The Birth of the Prison* (trans by Alan Sheridan; UK: Penguin, 1991), 196.

7 Yuval Noah Harari, "the world after coronavirus," (20 March 2020). https://www.ft.com/content/19d90308-6858-11ea-a3c9-1fe6fedcca75

8 For Agamben, coronavirus is a human 'invention', and it is just another version of flu. I do not subscribe to both views in this book.

9 Giorgio Agamben, "The state of exception provoked by an unmotivated emergency," (26 February 2020).

http://positionswebsite.org/giorgio-agamben-the-state-of-exception-provoked-by-an-unmotivated-emergency/#comment-93

10 Žižek, *Pandemic,* 84-5

[11] Giorgio Agamben, "The state of exception provoked by an unmotivated emergency," (26 February 2020).

http://positionswebsite.org/giorgio-agamben-the-state-of-exception-provoked-by-an-unmotivated-emergency/#comment-93

[12] Jean-Luc Nancy, "*Viral Exception*," (27 February 2020). http://www.journal-psychoanalysis.eu/coronavirus-and-philosophers/

[13] Giorgio Agamben, *Homo Sacer: Sovereign Power and Bare Life* (trans by Daniel Heller-Roazen; California: Stanford University Press, 1998), 4.

[14] Giorgio Shani, "Securitizing 'Bare Life'? Human Security and Coronavirus," (3 April 2020).

https://www.e-ir.info/2020/04/03/securitizing-bare-life-human-security-and coronavirus/?fbclid=IwAR2qNlK1SJl4uDIHQDj9inwAaQPkbEvigWaL_0JMQq39fTTm5WsegpN_Uaw

[15] Amartya Sen, "Overcoming a pandemic may look like fighting a war, but the real need is far from that," (8 April 2020). https://indianexpress.com/article/opinion/columns/coronavirus-india-lockdown-amartya-sen-economy-migrants-6352132/

[16] P. Thirumal, "India's Dalits Search for a Democratic Opening in the Digital Divide," https://www.academia.edu/37042178/India_s_Dalits_Search_for_a_Democratic_Opening_in_the_Digital_Divide?auto=download

[17] Matthew M. Cappiello, "COVID-19 Must Radicalize Doctors: We Cannot Remain on the Political Periphery," (27 April 2020). https://truthout.org/articles/covid-19-must-radicalize-doctors-we-cannot-remain-on-the-political-periphery/

[18] In fact, the word 'ubuntu' is just part of the Zulu phrase "Umuntu ngumuntu ngabantu", which literally means that a person is a person through other people. Ubuntu has its roots in humanist African philosophy, where the idea of community is one of the building blocks of society.

[19] Nitzan Lebovic and Daniel Weidner, "Prophetic Politics: an introduction," (21 April 2020). https://politicaltheology.com/prophetic-politics-an-introduction/?fbclid=IwAR1AqE0stIP3LLdy7iGyb_fwUWuwBT-LIzhKsv_NXG3fmGM5xcDalm6SivE

Chapter 4

Double Pandemic: COVID-19 and the Pandemic of Domestic Violence

Lockdown can't mean that you save me from a virus, but you expose me to other forms of violence.

Vrinda Grover, a senior Advocate and women's rights activist

COVID-19 is deepening existing inequalities, including gender inequality. Already we are seeing a reversal in decades of limited and fragile progress on gender equality and women's rights. And without a concerted response, we risk losing a generation or more of gains.

UN Secretary-General António Guterres

Introduction

"We're all in this together" and "we will come through this together" are the common refrains during the COVID pandemic. Who are this "we"? While it is true that the entire world is affected by COVID, the health risks, burdens, experiences and outcomes are not the same for everyone. "For many women, 'Stay Home, Stay Safe' means nothing as 'safe' and 'home' are not synonymous."[1] The UN has described the worldwide increase in domestic abuse as a "shadow pandemic" alongside COVID. It is the result of a "millennia of patriarchy." UN warns that the pandemic will likely disproportionately and devastatively affect women, exacerbate pre-existing gendered risks and vulnerabilities, and widen inequalities. When only impacts on women or men are considered, there is a risk of homogenising diverse experiences and reducing analysis to the simplistic message that "pandemics affect women and men differently." A narrow gender focus can reinforce binary and competing understandings of the burden posed by COVID on women versus men.

Fuelled by mandatory stay-at-home rules, physical distancing, economic uncertainties and anxieties caused by the pandemic, domestic violence has increased worldwide. During the first four phases of the COVID-related lockdown since 24 March 2020, Indian women filed more domestic violence complaints than recorded in a similar period in the last 10 years. The term "domestic violence" is used in many countries to refer to intimate partner violence, but it also encompasses child and elder abuse, and abuse by any member of a household. But even this unusual spurt is only the tip of the iceberg as 86 per cent women who experience domestic violence do not seek help in India. Data released by the National Commission for Women (NCW) in India showed a twofold increase in gender-based violence from March 2020 to April 2020. Globally, too, countries including China, the US, the UK, Brazil, Tunisia, France, Australia and others reported cases of increased domestic violence and intimate partner violence. In South Africa alone, the first week of the lockdown witnessed 90,000 reports of violence against women. In Malaysia and China, distress calls doubled.

Lockdown or Lock Up?: Gender Virus 'Inside' and Coronavirus 'Outside'

MASK-19 is not the brand name of a face mask to protect against and limit the spread of COVID. It is not a postmodern buzzword either. MASCARILLA-19 (MASK-19) is the name of an initiative in Spain, started on 30 March 2020, to support women facing violence during the pandemic by providing a safe place to report abuse. The idea was originally mooted by Kika Fumero of the Canary Islands Institute for Equality and promoted by the Andalusia Women's Institute (IAM). Reaching out to the victims of gender-based domestic violence is classified as an essential service in Spain. When a woman experiences violence at home or sexual assault, she can head to the nearest medical store and simply use the code word MASK-19 to the pharmacy staff. Asking for MASK-19 is being used as a code for people who cannot speak openly to indicate that they are being abused and are seeking help. Inspired by Spain, France, Germany, Italy, Norway and Argentina have adopted a similar scheme for victims to report violence at the nearest drugstore with the code MASK-19.

The UN Conference on Trade and Development makes an important observation about the pandemic using a gender lens: "The impact of the COVID-19 pandemic is not gender neutral, as it affects men and women differently." Therefore, we must not be gender blind in our responses to the pandemic, or else women will carry a disproportionately higher economic cost than men. Globally, women are more vulnerable to economic shocks wrought by crises such as the coronavirus pandemic. The conference concluded that the following five reasons put women more at risk during this crisis:[2]

1. The service sector is hit hard by the restrictions imposed to manage the spread of the coronavirus. Given that some 55 per cent of women are employed in the service sector (compared with 44 per cent of men), women are more likely to be adversely affected. Moreover, female-dominated service sectors such as food, hospitality and tourism are among those expected to feel the harshest economic effects of the measures to contain the spread of the pandemic.

2. Women entrepreneurs are often discriminated against when attempting to access credit. This will be a challenge as credit will be of paramount importance for surviving the current crisis. Without open and favourable lines of credit, many female entrepreneurs will be forced to close their businesses.

3. Women's unpaid work is set to increase. Women remain responsible for the lion's share of domestic chores and care work. Measures to contain the pandemic such as quarantines and closure of schools imply additional household work and responsibility for them. Some women would be forced to make difficult decisions to leave the labour market or opt for part-time jobs, as juggling between caring for family members and paid work becomes untenable.

4. According to the International Labour Organisation, across the world, out of the less than 40 per cent of total employment women represent, they constitute 57 per cent of those working on a part-time basis. As the effects of the COVID-19 pandemic roll through economies, reducing employment opportunities and

triggering layoffs, temporary workers, the majority of them women, bear the heaviest brunt of job losses.

5. Social safety nets mostly depend upon a formal participation in the labour force. But since women tend to work without clear terms of employment, they often are not entitled to reliable social protection such as health insurance, paid sick and maternity leave, pensions and unemployment benefits. In many developing countries, women are either self-employed or work as contributing family workers, for example in family farms. In South Asia, over 80 per cent of women in non-agricultural jobs are in informal employment; in sub-Saharan Africa this figure is 74 per cent; and in Latin America and the Caribbean, 54 per cent of women in non-agricultural jobs participate in informal employment.

Reports and data suggest that COVID becomes the perfect soil for "intimate terrorism"— a term many experts prefer for domestic violence. Home gets more violent and abusive than ever in the swiftly fluctuating lockdown landscape. Mandatory stay-at-home rules, disease distancing, economic uncertainties and stress caused by the pandemic worsen the stress for gender-motivated perpetrators to the extent of abusing women for slight reasons. Stress makes abusers even more volatile, while heightened privacy gives them a feeling of impunity. BBC reporter Natalie Higgins puts it well, "Women fear the aggressor inside the home and the virus outside."[3]

UN Secretary-General Antonio Guterres warned against a "horrifying surge in domestic violence" due to mounting uncertainties and burdens as lockdowns and quarantines take effect around the world. "I recently called for an immediate global ceasefire to focus on our shared struggle to overcome the pandemic…. But violence is not confined to the battlefield. For many women and girls, the threat looms largest where they should be safest: in their own homes."[4] Meanwhile, the UN Population Fund Deputy Director Dr Ramiz Alakbarov has said that there could be an extra 61 million cases of gender-based violence if lockdowns were to continue for a year.[5]

Global reports concerning domestic abuse clearly indicate that there is a dramatic spike in "another pandemic" within a pandemic. NGOs in Argentina that have been monitoring gender violence have estimated that was a doubling in the number of femicides every day in the short span of one month into the lockdown. London's Metropolitan Police said it had carried out over 4,000 domestic abuse arrests in the first six weeks of the country's lockdown, and that calls relating to domestic abuse had risen by about a third. In France, within a week police reports of domestic abuse had gone up nationally by a third, and by even more in Paris. Between March and April, the National Commission of Women (NCW) in India received 310 grievances of domestic violence and 885 complaints for other forms of violence against women.

Domestic violence against women is a "pandemically horrid reality" and a "ticking bomb." One might say that violence happening behind closed doors is purely a private matter and beyond the scope of public scrutiny because "there is no CCTV at home," as Deborah Orr cynically puts it.[6] The patriarchal mindset that dismisses domestic violence as a private matter between intimate partners must be challenged and problematised. Domestic violence is not a private issue. It is a social and political issue. It is a moral issue. Domestic violence is a crime against the law. It is a criminal justice matter for various reasons. First and foremost, as CNN correspondent Sandra Horley opines, "violence is always a choice"[7] and therefore it is "preventable not inevitable."[8] Renowned trauma expert Judith Lewis Herman of Harvard University argues that the intimidating methods abusers use to control women "bear an uncanny resemblance" to those abductors use to control captives and brutal governments use to weaken political convicts mentally.[9] In other words, the perpetrators of "intimate terrorism" replicate the coercive methods of political and sexual exploitation.[10]

Second, the politics of domestic violence compels us to look at the pandemic through a gendered lens. Various systems of power relations make women weaker and vulnerable. All these patriarchal systems of power habitually work on various fault lines such as feminisation of work, poverty, reproductive health, financial constraints, purity and pollution dogmas, male chauvinistic religious practices, and education. When all these factors intersect, the lives of women become more powerless and repressive. Economic insecurity plays a crucial part in this intersectionality.

Third, the gendering of space is another root cause of increasing domestic violence during this time of the invisible "bio tyrant." The characteristic patriarchal divide between public and private, where public space is for men and private spheres are for women, is intersecting during these trying times. Coerced intersection of hitherto opposite public and private spheres during the so-called "great sabbatical" requires the coexistence of the abuser and the abused. As "homemakers" in quarantine, sexual division of labour increases the workload of women in taking care of household chores. Consequently, the private space traditionally defined as hers is now redrawn constantly in favour of patriarchal power configurations. It has and will have huge democratic ramifications as it normalises sexual division of labour, and the intersectionality of gender and politics of violence.

According to Rukmini Sen, Professor in sociology at Ambedkar University, Delhi, "there is also a need to re-conceptualise the home/domesticity itself."[11] The assumed traditional binary of women's lives between the two spaces of the maternal home or the matrimonial home have definitely limited the possibilities of a discourse around a safe, liveable, affordable, domestic space for any woman. While economic independence is definitely a pre-requisite for this, however, it is not sufficient to even imagine a space like that at the cost of either of those homes. There is a need to start talking about a different kind of shared/collective residences (not connected only to marriage). It is therefore relevant to raise discussions around affordable civic/community, abuse-free secure, liveable housing, not connected with marriage. The discussion on domestic violence can no longer continue to happen in isolation from rethinking the discourse surrounding gendering of home/space/domesticity.

The consequences of the coronavirus pandemic have laid bare the extreme social divisions in India based on Brahminical patriarchy and caste hierarchy. That is, Dalit women suffer multiple forms of discrimination—as Dalits, as the poor and as women. Gender disparities sharpen during calamities and conflicts, making the burden worse. From the way one dresses and lives to the way in which once earns a living and makes a livelihood, caste is a compelling dictator which commands everything, including this virus. It is caste-based jobs such as scavenging and sanitation, their subsequent minimal social values, and inadequate remuneration leading to unhygienic slum lifestyles that expose Dalit and Adivasi communities to the fatal risks of COVID-19.

While migrant labourers and workers from the unorganised sector have been ignored in general by policymakers, women among them have it worse. Many have been evicted from their homes, lost their jobs and face an uncertain impact on their livelihoods. Women working in the unorganised sector, street vendors and daily wagers, including domestic workers, have had to face great repercussions from loss of their livelihoods in the wake of the pandemic. Apart from losing incomes and being evicted from homes, they face the additional threat of sexual harassment.

Diakonia as Gender-Equal Initiatives and Ekklēsia as Gynocritical Space

The lockdown on the one hand has ensured the safety of lakhs of Indians from coronavirus, but on the other hand, it means worsened living conditions and frequent abuse for a lot of people. The period of lockdown has seen a steep increase in the cases of domestic violence and other gendered violence. Only gender-equal initiatives can save the ecology of economy and the dignity of women. Support measures in response to COVID-19 should go beyond workers who hold formal employment and include informal, part-time and seasonal workers, most of whom are women. This is particularly necessary in female-dominated work spheres such as the hospitality, food and tourism sectors, now at a standstill due to confinement measures by governments. Some countries are already moving in this direction to retain women's productive participation in the labour force. For example, Italy is considering putting into place support measures to cover informal and temporary workers once their contracts are over.[12]

Prime Minister Giuseppe Conte is preparing an unprecedented emergency stimulus package worth 30 billion euros ($33 billion) for workers trapped in Italy's underground economy.

For women, imperial invasions and colonisations are not different from the pandemic. When the Roman Emperor Claudius expelled all Jews from Rome, Priscilla and Aquila, an early missionary couple, along with thousands of Jews, left as refugees and settled in Corinth (Acts 18:2-3). Just as this pandemic is forcing women to do, new material realities must have redrawn the lifeworld of Priscilla. In Priscilla, we see an intersection of various issues such as gender, race and class. But Priscilla found a radical way to challenge patriarchal patronage and conservatism by making tents as a means of sustenance (Acts 18:1-3).

Economic liberation and independence are very important to gender justice. This gender-equal response to the forced geographical relocation and the subsequent material resistance made her equipped to be an entrepreneur, a travelling evangelist (Acts 18:18), a teacher (Acts 18:24-28), a church planter and as one known for intellectual engagement. Priscilla is certainly not Aquila's property, as was customary in Graeco-Roman society, but rather his partner in ministry and marriage. It is possible the ekklēsial gathering in the house helped Priscilla transcend the stereotypical division between community and household in the Greaco-Roman sphere. "The public sphere of the Christian community was *in* the house and not outside of the household. The community was 'in her house.' Therefore, it seems that the *domina* of the house, where the ecclesia gathered, had primary responsibility for the community *and* its gathering in the house church [emphasis original]."[13] Priscilla reclaims her agency and identity through economic liberation.

We have many Priscillas among rural women in India. An entrepreneurial wave across the country since the COVID-19 crisis has spurred rural women in India to act.[14]Swayam Shikshan Prayog (SSP) is a non-profit training programme for rural woman in the drought-prone Marathwada belt of Maharashtra to adopt climate-smart and drought-resistant farm practices. Many of these women saw COVID-19 as an opportunity to use their insights to prepare their communities for the long battle ahead and to steer them through the impending food crisis. Arogya Sakhis, self-help groups (SHGs) and community leaders, in partnership with the SSP and frontline government workers, are helping vulnerable families in rural villages by creating awareness about prevention, hygiene, social distancing, combating stigma, and providing dry food and hygiene essentials.

Tribal women of Odisha's Sundergarh district turned Good Samaritans amid the pandemic. Despite carrying on with their lives in simple circumstances and amongst harder struggles, 12 tribal women produced face masks for the poor and spread awareness on the impact of COVID-19 in three gram panchayats of Sundergarh district in Odisha.[15] They Knowing tailoring, they could independently make nearly 500 masks within a week which was otherwise inaccessible and unaffordable for the villagers. All these women are associated with the Mahila Sangram Samiti, a people's collective that works for the socio-economic and political empowerment of the marginalised communities, and especially for women, in Sundergarh. As getting raw materials for making masks was an arduous task during the lockdown, they decided to donate their new sarees for making masks.

Conclusion
The COVID-19 pandemic has brought to the fore another crisis triggered by the lockdown—that of increasing cases of

domestic violence against women locked in abusive homes and circumstances. The gynocritical initiatives of the Priscillas from rural India in the face of COVID guarantee women their agency and advocacy. This is crucial as women's autonomy in a patriarchal domestic space is reduced when homes become spaces to earn livelihood during the lockdown; homes are evolving as spaces where people are working from home. In a deeply patriarchal society such as ours, members of the family expect everything to be as it is on any "normal" day. In such a context of possible violence, diakonia means initiating or partnering with gender-equal responses of women such as those by rural women in such as those in Odisha and Maharashtra in India or movements like MASK-19 globally. Only financially independent Priscillas can repossess their agency and dignity both in the *oikia* space and in the public space; diakonia for women in the age of coronavirus means reclaiming their ontological and political agency. This makes a faith community an inclusive space of irreducible gender differences, called ekklēsia.

Endnotes

[1] Girija Shivakumar, "While Battling COVID-19, We Can't Let the Pandemic of Domestic Violence continue," 16 April 2020). https://thewire.in/women/covid-19-lockdown-domestic-violence

[2] Isabelle Durant, "COVID-19 requires gender-equal responses to save economies," (1 April 2020). https://unctad.org/en/pages/newsdetails.aspx?OriginalVersionID=2319

[3] Natalie Higgins, "Coronavirus: When home gets violent under lockdown in Europe," (13 April 2020). https://www.bbc.com/news/world-europe-52216966

[4] https://news.un.org/en/story/2020/04/1061052 (6 April 2020).

[5] António Guterres, "COVID-19 is the greatest test that we have faced since the formation of the United Nations," (June 2020). https://www.unfpa.

org/sites/default/files/resource-pdf/UNFPA_Global_Response_Plan_Revised_June_2020_.pdf (June 2020).

[6] Deborah Orr, "Is domestic violence a private matter because there's no CCTV at home?," (13 July 2020). https://www.theguardian.com/commentisfree/2013/jul/13/domestic-violence-private-matter-cctv

[7] Sandra Horley, "Why domestic violence is never a private issue," (19 June 2013). https://edition.cnn.com/2013/06/19/opinion/opinion-domestic-violence-not-private-issue/index.html

[8] https://unric.org/en/who-warns-of-surge-of-domestic-violence-as-covid-19-cases-decrease-in-europe/ (5 May 2020).

[9] Amanda Taub, "A New Covid-19 Crisis: Domestic Abuse Rises Worldwide," (14 April 2020). https://www.nytimes.com/2020/04/06/world/coronavirus-domestic-violence.html

[10] Judith Lewis Herman, "Complex PTSD: A Syndrome in Survivors of Prolonged and Repeated Trauma," *Journal of Traumatic Stress*, Vol 5, No. 3 (1992): 377–391.

[11] Rukmini Sen, "Stay Home, Stay Safe: Interrogating Violence in the Domestic Sphere," (23 June 2020).

[12] John Follain, "Italy Readies Emergency Cash for Workers in Underground Economy," (31 March 2020). https://www.bloomberg.com/news/articles/2020-03-31/italy-readies-emergency-cash-for-workers-in-underground-economy

[13] Elisabeth Schiissler Fiorenza, *In Memory of her: A Feminist Theological Reconstruction of Christian Origins* (New York: Crossroad, 1994), 176.

[14] Moin Qazi, "Rural Women Respond to Covid-19 With Great Enterprise," (23 April 2020). https://countercurrents.org/2020/04/rural-women-respond-to-covid-19-with-great-enterprise/

[15] Naba Kishor Pujari, "Tribal women of Odisha's Sundergarh district turn Good Samaritans in tackling COVID 19," (23 April 2020). https://countercurrents.org/2020/04/tribal-women-of-odishas-sundergarh-district-turn-good-samaritans-in-tackling-covid-19/

Chapter 5

Migrant Labourers and Pandemic Apartheid

When lockdown is not ending & Govt is not facilitating our travel, we've no option but to walk. If we die here, our mortal remains will also not reach our homes.

Rajkumari, member of a migrant family
from Sitapur in Uttar Pradesh

I will not come back here even if I have to beg at home. This is no life.

Anil Soni, a house painter by profession

Introduction

India saw an unparalleled loss of jobs for migrant labourers over the course of the first nationwide "genocidal lockdown" imposed in the last week of March 2020. Tens of thousands of daily-wage migrant workers now faced a pandemic apartheid in the city they have helped build and run. So, with the impending fear of poverty and hunger, the workers began a gruelling exodus to their villages ("reverse exodus")—walking, cycling and hitching rides on lorries, trucks and even water tankers.

Many had to travel thousands of kilometres to "go home." As many as 80 migrants died of starvation and heat stroke while making the perilous journey home. At least 198 migrants were killed and 1,390 injured in road accidents during their journey as on 30 May 2020, according to data compiled by the road safety NGO Save LIFE Foundation.

Pandemic of Migrant Exodus, Xenophobia and 'Chemical Solution'

India's nationwide lockdown critically dislocated and 'invisibilised' its migrant population. Lacking jobs and money, and with public transportation shut down, thousands of migrants were forced to walk back to their home villages in the hinterland. When faced with an imminent threat to life, they thought family was a much stronger factor than an urban occupation. They, though, were not homeward bound to seek material help from their family in the village; what disturbed them profoundly was the fear of dying alone with nobody to perform the last rites for them. "In a sense, this is a refugee crisis now and not merely a migrant crisis," Irudaya Rajan said.

Many of these migrant workers were thrown into a gyre of uncertainty and suffering. Some were stripped of their dignity as officials unceremoniously sprayed and doused them with a 'chemical solution' to disinfect them. Some were beaten up and asked to turn back for fear of spreading the virus to far-flung, rural and remote parts of the country. This state-backed brand of brutality and vigilante justice only catalysed further paranoia and fear-mongering and raised questions of human rights.

The struggles of migrant workers, once again, revealed a deeply-rooted intersectional problem of conflict, particularly bringing to the fore deeply-rooted issues like xenophobia. Migrant workers faced xenophobic biases and were often treated like "outsiders." This period also revealed pointed racism and discrimination against north-eastern Indians in the rest of India. While they have been routinely mocked for their language, food and culture, the pandemic saw them being called "Coronavirus" and thrown out of houses for "looking Chinese."

Women from the north-eastern states have faced widespread discrimination and harassment. They were attacked with racial slurs and targeted for supposedly spreading the virus. A man on a bike spat on a Manipuri woman in Delhi's Vijay Nagar area before calling out "Chinese coronavirus coming." Another woman who hails from the region and her friend were hit with water balloons and called "Coronavirus" by two men on a bike near Delhi University's North Campus. Female migrant workers were unable to get essential supplies, including sanitary products. In addition, female daily-wage labourers and agricultural workers in the country, already underpaid, lost their jobs and daily pay.

Moreover, workers from Jharkhand and Bihar who made it back home were turned away from their own villages and subject to health checks. Some villages even erected barricades out of fear of the transmission of the virus. Many lost their lives on the way home during the punitive lockdown. BBC correspondent Vikas Pandey reported many such instances.[1] In desperation during the lockdown, Sanju Yadav and her husband, Rajan, and their two children, Nitin and Nandini, decided to undertake the 1,500 km long journey in their *tuk-tuk*. The family of four left Mumbai on 09 May 2020. But in the early hours of 12 May—just 200km from their village—a truck rammed into the *tuk-tuk* from behind. Lallu Ram began the journey on foot with four friends to his village in Uttar Pradesh's Allahabad district, some 1,400 km away. They covered around 400 km in the first 48 hours, hitchhiking on lorries. But Lallu died of cardiac arrest, triggered by exhaustion and fatigue.

Similarly, two tailors from Bihar, Sagheer and Sahib Ansari, decided to go back to their village in Motihari district in Bihar, some 1,200 km from Delhi. After riding a cycle for five days, their group reached Lucknow, the capital of Uttar Pradesh. It had been two days since they had a proper meal and were surviving on puffed rice. A car came out of nowhere, hitting the barrier and striking Sagheer. He died in hospital a few hours later. Sahib said: "I don't know who to blame for his death—coronavirus, hunger or poverty. I have understood one thing: I will never leave my village. I will make less money but at least I will stay alive."

Perhaps the most brutal incident in India was in Aurangabad, Maharashtra. Sixteen migrant labourers, who were walking along the railway tracks to catch the "Shramik Special" train to go home, were run over by a freight train. After walking for several hours, the exhausted workers sat down to rest and slept off on the tracks, assuming that trains were not running due to lockdown. An oncoming cargo train ran over then at 5.20 a.m.

According to the Business & Human Rights Resource Centre,[2] the predicament of migrant labourers is not significantly different in other parts of the world. As the high season for agricultural labour in the United States approached, tens of thousands of migrant workers from Mexico were getting ready to head to the fields in their northern neighbour to carry out work that ensures that food makes it to people's tables. But with the US having the most COVID infections in the world had worsened the already precarious conditions in which these workers plant, harvest, process and transport fruits and vegetables. The Jordanian Council of Ministers issued a new order regulating the relationship between the private sector and workers amid the pandemic. The new order obliged employers to renew fixed-term contracts only for Jordanian workers. Hundreds of thousands of Central Asian migrants got trapped in Russia's quarantine lockdown, lacking jobs, livelihoods and free access to healthcare. They were already subjected to xenophobia and discrimination in Russia long before COVID arrived.

In a significant development, even as many anxious migrants were trying to get back to their hometowns, a few state governments tried to stop them from returning. The Karnataka government in India put a hold on "unnecessary" interstate movement of migrant workers as it wanted to resume construction and other industrial activities.[3] Delhi Chief Minister Arvind Kejriwal appealed to migrant workers to not leave the city as he also wanted to resume "in situ construction" work and factories.[4] P. Sainath's comments on the migrant crisis is very poignant: "You're suddenly finding a lot of sectors hamstrung by the disappearance of the migrant labour that made them. So, the country is beginning to figure out who its workforce is. And it's not the bright boys of Bengaluru."[5]

Genocidal Lockdown and Permanent Epidemic of Untouchability

In the view of Jeane Dreze, Belgian-born Indian economist and social scientist, the real and the main reason behind the government's reluctance and resistance to allow migrant workers to return to their villages is that employers do not want to lose their "pool of cheap labour."[6] This harsh decision to forbid workers from going back is a "death sentence". Dreze said all decisions and policies made to contain the pandemic had been made or influenced by a "privileged class of people who are far more afraid of contracting the infection themselves than they are concerned about the consequences of the lockdown for poor people."[7] For such people who pay little attention to the underprivileged, "human decency is an outdated speed bump on the road to development and self-reliance"; therefore, development demands "the funeral of human decency."[8]

While this fear of losing a pool of cheap labour is the ostensible reason for governments stopping migrant labourers from returning, there is more to it. For migrant labourers and Dalits more deadly than the virus is caste. As Jeya Rani puts it, "An invisible virus highlights the virulence of an age-old visible virus."[9] If "social distancing" between persons is a non-discriminatory mandate for curbing the spread of the coronavirus, "do not touch" (untouchability) has been a *cordon sanitaire*—roping off a whole community—for Dalits in the name of religious practices. We have two clearly demarcated Indias—one that is "touchable" (rich India) and the other that is its very opposite, or 'untouchable' (poor India).

Caste is a permanent epidemic spread by the "touchables" in India. While the lockdown has resulted in restricted lives for these 'touchables', it has not fundamentally altered or threatened the socio-economic fabric of their existence. But what of the other India, which comprises two-thirds of a population of 135 crore? The social isolation, or untouchability, that has pushed a significant section of this India into a bottomless pit of poverty for centuries is now assuming a different form to punish them economically, snatching from them their last remaining wherewithal to survive. Those prohibited from entering the streets of the dominant castes due to caste discrimination now find themselves barred from all streets due to the lockdown. Has

India ever thought about "de-castifying" itself just as the Germans de-Nazified themselves after the World War II?

The pandemic has exposed the hypocritical attitude of various other countries, such as the US, towards migrant workers. There are economic compulsions behind the federal government's unofficial decision to temporarily change the "hit-the-immigrant-like-a-piñata policy" and deem hitherto "illegal" workers as a category of "essential" superheroes in the face of the pandemic.[10] Various states realised that food security, especially frontline sectors such as fieldwork or farm work, meatpacking and delivery, cannot be disconnected from the issue of border security. This necessitates legalising the status of all essential workers in the country. Joe L. Del Bosque of Del Bosque Farms, one of the largest organic melon growers in the US, said: "Sadly, it's taken a pandemic for Americans to realize that the food in their grocery stores, on their tables, is courtesy of mostly Mexican workers, the majority of them without documents…. They're the most vulnerable of workers. They're not hiding behind the pandemic waiting for a stimulus check."[11]

COVID-19 is also a pandemic of hatred, exclusionism and violence. At the heart of this "pandemic of xenophobia" are migrant labourers and refugees struggling to negotiate their way through the incomparable crisis.[12] Amnesty International has warned that a secondary pandemic of misrepresentation, misinformation, hate speech and scapegoating of people perceived to be "outsiders"—both online and offline—could alarmingly worsen the anti-migrant rhetoric and subsequently increase violence against those who are vulnerable and seeking safety. "They (migrants and refugees) have unique challenges due to their legal and immigration status, precarious work situations, and restricted access to public benefits and health care systems. Their experiences are complicated by language and cultural barriers, xenophobia, racism, discrimination, stigma and exclusion," says a recent Amnesty observation piece.[13]

In India, xenophobic rhetoric vilifies and stigmatises even citizens of the country as migrants or outsiders. People who do white-collar jobs change jobs and move to different cities for better prospects. Central government officers and defence service personnel keep changing cities frequently. But no one calls them migrants. But a significant population from Indian villages working in cities are called migrants and denied dignity and an identity. Is this workforce of nation-builders not citizens of India? Are they outsiders? By ominously defining them as migrants, we deny them human dignity and push them towards a meaningless identity and an elusive future.

This clarifies why the "ecology of coronavirus" discourse often slide into "economy of the nation." Leaders in countries like India, US, Brazil and the UK do not seem to care if reactions to COVID-19 is taking us to an Orwellian world, displaying a sort of 'herd mentality' among them. Akin to herd immunity in medical terms, the exponents of 'community immunity' theory argue that economic collapse must be averted even if the virus is left free to circulate, threatening the lives of the most vulnerable people. In the new quasi-Aryan community, the poor and Dalits are not valued lives, and if they die, that is apparently acceptable, since they are not imagined as productive workers, but "drains" on the economy.

But "social Darwinism' is not possible because COVID spreads fast, patients can be asymptomatic and surviving the disease provides no immunity. The notion of "social immunity" mentioned above is a neoliberal economic agenda to throw the "expendable" people to death and poverty. If the vulnerable class wants to be "protected" by staying out of the workplace, the result is the intensification of unemployment. Even otherwise, the poor cannot afford to stay home. The poor are erased from the imagination of neoliberals and capitalists functioning along a neo-Malthusian line of "necessary loss" of a section of population in the time of an epidemic (or a war) and those powers who uphold the cause of life.[14]

Diakonia as Collaboration, and Ekklēsia as Collaborative Space

Instead of political stunts and cheap theatrics, diakonia in the context of the pandemic apartheid and the subsequent funeral of human decency means a "collaboration with labour movements."[15] Faith communities cannot do it with their customary tools and approaches alone. They need to engage in fruitful, collaborative and long-haul relationships with strategic social movement partners committed to the work of justice. One major obstacle for this collaboration is that, for the most part, faith communities and labour unions operate in entirely different silos. The handful of faith leaders, worshiping communities and organising networks that are directly engaged in the question of labour are an exception. This is despite the long tradition of faith and labour moments in US history—from Dr. Martin Luther King Jr.'s final act of solidarity with striking sanitation workers in Memphis, which had its roots in an important faith and labour coalition, to the National Farm Worker Ministry that emerged out of the United Farm Workers organising in California. Today, these events are understood primarily as moments in history. As a result, rarely would religious communities speak of labour justice or engage in discussions about class.

The parable of the workers in the vineyard may be seen in this context (Matt 2:1–16). Contrary to usual practice, the owner going out many times a day to hire unemployed labourers shows oversupply and unemployment. But the owner is doing this on a daily basis, avoiding long-term contracts. Daily-wage labourers were a common sight in the marketplace (Matt 20:3). As a result, the workers not only suffered from unemployment and poverty but also became "expendable" or 'involuntary marginals' of a cheap pool of labour for the urban elite. The labourers could not dispute the offered wage but agreed on a denarius a day (Matt 20:2), which was just enough for daily sustenance.

However, the payment process (Matt 20:9-10) is an egalitarian gesture of solidarity; the owner pays all the workers a day's wage and treats all as equal, which echoes Matt 19:17. The owner of the vineyard ensures minimum income and daily work for all those looking for means of sustenance. Jesus' father Joseph was also a migrant worker in Egypt. On their return from Egypt, Joseph settled in Nazareth, which was not his hometown. Being the son of a migrant worker, Jesus knew the economic struggles of the families of migrant workers. This must have certainly informed Jesus' theological interventions in the life of migrant workers in the first-century Roman-controlled Jewish homeland.

There are two possibilities for the owner's generosity—either the owner is generous by himself or is compelled to be generous because of union or voluntary organisations. The latter is more likely as the Roman world had many voluntary associations, and workers could protest over their wages or working conditions. According to *Bava Metziah* (Talmudic Aramaic), the second of the first three Talmudic tractates in the order of Nezikin ("Damages"), which discusses civil matters such as property law and usury: "The wool workers and the dyers are permitted to say, 'We will all be partners in any business that comes to the city.' The bakers are permitted to establish work shifts amongst themselves. Donkey drivers are permitted to say, 'We will provide another donkey for anyone whose donkey dies'…. The shipmasters are permitted to say, 'We will provide another ship for anyone whose ship is destroyed'" (11.24–26).

God's "domestic solidarity" with the migrant labourers is also comprehensively evident in the book of Exodus.[16] The people of Israel were "illegal workers/slaves" in Egypt. But the Pharaoh did not let them go because they were a cheap workforce. Their sweat and tears were the "essential raw material" for the Pharaoh to build his state and storehouses; the Pharaoh's empire stands on this "expendable-essential force" and their materiality. In the same vein, thousands of workers from various countries have built the modern cities around the world. But the lockdown and quarantine protocols and their impact for migrant workers and daily-wage labourers are tragically different. They have found themselves lost on the streets, jobless and homeless.

Conclusion

As a faith community, diakonia in the context of the pandemic is to practice domestic solidarity with the political society and thus interrogate the myopia of political institutions. Following the distinction made by India's leading social scientist Partha Chatterjee, migrant labourers and the unorganised working force are excluded from civil society, which is constituted of the urban middle class.[17] Civil society is the sphere in which urban middle class individuals carry out their life transactions and routines without difficulties during the lockdown and are able to work from home. They are backed by most social institutions and the rule of law. Political society, on the other hand, is constituted by the vast majority of the floating population of the dispossessed and displaced. They have democratic/voting rights, but no political rights or the privileges of society. If the literal meaning of the term ekklēsia is political gathering, then it must be domestic solidarity with the political society to make daily justice for the jobless and the homeless a reality.

> As daily bread is necessary
> So is daily justice.
> It is even necessary several times a day.
>
> From morning till night, at work, enjoying oneself.
> At work which is an enjoyment.
> In hard times and in happy times
> The people require the plentiful, wholesome
> Daily bread of justice.
>
> Since the bread of justice, then, is so important
> Who, friends, shall bake it?
>
> (Bertolt Brecht, "The Bread of the People")

Endnotes

[1] Vikas Pandey, "Coronavirus lockdown: The Indian migrants dying to get home," (20 May 2020). https://www.bbc.com/news/world-asia-india-52672764

[2] https://www.business-humanrights.org/en

[3] Christin Mathew Philip, "Covid-19: Karnataka urges migrants to stay back, halts train," (6 May 2020). https://timesofindia.indiatimes.com/city/bengaluru/karnataka-government-puts-inter-state-migrant-train-travel-on-hold/articleshow/75566034.cms

[4] Sourav Roy Barman, https://indianexpress.com/article/cities/delhi/arvind-kejriwal-delhi-covid-19-cases-migrant-workers-lockdown6402987/ (11 May 2020).

[5] https://scroll.in/video/961301/indias-workforce-is-not-the-bright-boys-of-bengaluru-journalist-p-sainath-on-the-migrant-crisis (16 August 2020).

[6] https://scroll.in/latest/960758/covid-19-host-states-dont-want-to-lose-cheap-labour-claims-jean-dreze-on-migrant-crisis?fbclid=IwAR1NWU_2i4_

tz-9q0c6sdAUrtDBMuJOmyWC4LQEZBXYrMXscvuUDrIkKihc (16 August 2020).

7 https://www.newindianexpress.com/nation/2020/apr/28/the-jean-dreze-interview-keeping-migrant-workers-from- returning-home-will-deepen-covid-19-financial—2136066.html?fbclid=IwAR0OL5iW4ybS_DVPpS0XAaN_efxvYiJOwS97g1MLzlhk7n2xDD8UKpHdpr4 (28 April 2020).

8 https://www.deccanherald.com/opinion/the-funeral-of-human-decency-838544.html?fbclid=IwAR2TnH2coks_F4OuuVSRCunJC87 BNBlNUUkyw5CrNoSoKxCuE26buNJ0-Q0

9 Jeya Rani, "An Invisible Virus Highlights the Virulence of an Age-Old Visible Virus," (14 April 2020). https://thewire.in/caste/coronavirus-caste-discrimination-india

10 Alfredo Corchado, "A Former Farmworker on American Hypocrisy," (6 May 2020). https://www.nytimes.com/2020/05/06/opinion/sunday/coronavirus-essential-workers.html?fbclid=IwAR0v5wM1Hwl4w847tifGOs FA2zYdztZpLiVgLs5SnXC6-exU8CPi5zZK9BA

11 Alfredo Corchado, "A Former Farmworker on American Hypocrisy," (6 May 2020). https://www.nytimes.com/2020/05/06/opinion/sunday/coronavirus-essential-workers.html?fbclid=IwAR0v5wM1Hwl4w847tifGOs FA2zYdztZpLiVgLs5SnXC6-exU8CPi5zZK9BA

12 Ratna, "Pandemic of Xenophobia: The Outbreak & Our Migrants," (23 May 2020). https://empirediaries.com/2020/05/22/pandemic-of-xenophobia-the-outbreak-our-migrants/

13 Chiranjeevi Bhat, "The Shocking History of Amnesty International," (31 October 2018). http://indiafacts.org/the- shocking-history-of-amnesty-international/?fbclid=IwAR3PIR2wDJrTr-E6uj5R4sIKZWVg6oOmW6uwCwOH lFEZhtL5xhC_v8KjbyE

14 Monobina Gupta, Interview with Ranabir Samaddar (23 April 2020). https://thewire.in/rights/interview-ranabir-samaddar-migrant-workers-invisible

15 Francisco Garcia, "Faith Needs Labour to Respond to this Moment," (21 May 2020). https://www.religionandjustice.org/blog/faith-needs-labor-to-respond-to-this-moment?fbclid=IwAR0_QXFPReDoMwaRcN19Xz4kCW1o7ua_HZRp3hVYmusYB7F7K5s8DluUKw0

16 Sandeep Datta, "India: Migrant workers' plight prompts UN call for 'domestic solidarity' in coronavirus battle," (2 April 2020). https://news.un.org/en/story/2020/04/1060922

17 Rudrangshu Mukherjee, "Modi's myopia and indifference to the poor," (22 May 2020). https://standpointmag.co.uk/issues/may-june-2020/modis-myopia-and-indifference-to-the-poor/?fbclid=IwAR0dgWx59rmF3-Upm2e F14zLALI6h3CCFLpkQbNA0kzJb2qSTEEvYf47e9Q

Chapter 6

Republic of 'Hungervirus'

For the poor the fear is not the virus, but the hunger and employment that will kill them even without the Corona.

Vivek Sakpal

At least now those who say, 'The coronavirus does not discriminate, we are asking you to stay at home for your own safety,' should grasp the reality—between life and food, the marginalised will always choose food.

Jeya Rani

Introduction

"Virus means millions will be left in poverty," said World Bank President David Malpass.[1] Global poverty is set to rise over 100 million people once again as a result of the worst global crisis since World War II.[2] "Pandemic depression" is not just a social and economic crisis. It is also a humanitarian crisis as chronic poverty and its inter-generational transfer are becoming deadlier than the coronavirus. A study by King's College in London and the Australian National University points to poverty increasing dramatically in middle-income developing countries, where millions of people live just above the poverty line. Asian countries, such as Bangladesh, India, Indonesia, Pakistan and the Philippines, are considered to be particularly vulnerable to the pandemic's economic shockwaves, with lockdowns severely curtailing activity.

COVID-19 has further worsened India's hunger and malnutrition woes, more so for millions of informal workers on their way back home or struggling to make ends meet in their urban and rural homes. The embedded informality in labour, land and housing have uprooted and shaken them with loss of income, occupation and habitat, worsening their situation with regard to nutrition vulnerability. In India, with almost 90 per cent of its workforce in the informal economy, 400 million workers are at the risk of falling deeper into poverty during the crisis with "catastrophic consequences." This pandemic hunger is not the only worry. Post-COVID access to safe and nutritious food would be uncertain if adequate policy measures are not taken. Right, urgent measures could make the difference between survival and collapse.

Children too are affected by the economic and social consequences of lockdowns and other measures taken in the region to counter the pandemic. The South Asian region is likely to have around 360 million children pushed into poverty and food insecurity within the next six months, according to a UNICEF report released on 23 June 2020. Over 240 million children in the region were already classified as poor, but with the pandemic an additional 120 million children would likely be affected, said the report. South Asia is home to over 600 million children under 18 years of age, with nearly six out of every 10 of them likely to become poor and food insecure, according to UNICEF's estimates.

According to Jean Gough, UNICEF regional director for South Asia: "The side-effects of the pandemic across South Asia—including the lockdown and other measures—have been damaging for children in numerous ways. But the long-term impact of the economic crisis on children will be on a different scale entirely. Without urgent action now, COVID-19 could destroy the hopes and futures of an entire generation." At least 1.5 million children in Uttar Pradesh in India missed their vaccination doses due to the nationwide lockdown. In April 2020, Bangladesh reported a 49 per cent reduction in the number of children receiving routine vaccinations compared with March 2020. Within weeks of the lockdown, seven measles outbreaks and around 250 cases were reported in different parts of Nepal. "The direct risk to children from the virus is much less than that from the disruption to routine health services," said Paul Rutter, UNICEF's health adviser for South Asia. "It is crucial that childbirth, child health and nutrition services remain available for families during COVID-19," he added.

Hunger Pandemic: Buy Mask or Food?

Against the backdrop of COVID and its impact on millions of poor and migrant labourers, a heart-wrenching video that surfaced on social media—a famished labourer eating the raw meat of a dead dog on the Delhi-Jaipur National Highway in Shahpura, Rajasthan, India—sparked outrage.[3] The video was shot by a person who was on his way to Delhi. On seeing the man, he stopped his vehicle and asked him, "*Arre bhai kya hua, khana nahi hai tere pass* (do you not have food?)". The man making the video then asks him to get up and wait by the side of the road so he could give the poor man some food.

There are equally shocking incidents of the poor struggling against hunger. Journalist Narendra Nath Mishra shared tragic visuals that showed a violent scuffle between a group of emaciated and weather-worn migrant workers for a handful of biscuits.[4] In the wild scramble, some packets fall on the ground and are quickly picked up by alert hands. The incident allegedly took place at Katihar Junction, around 300 km from Bihar's capital Patna, as a train arrived from Delhi and stopped en route to Purnia. Daily visuals of thousands of poor people travelling hundreds of kilometres on foot and barely surviving on biscuits highlight the shocking extent of starvation and desperation on the highways of India amid the coronavirus lockdown.

Elsewhere, in central Asia, Hayatullah Khan, an Afghan labourer whose daily earnings fell below $1.50 during the coronavirus pandemic, had two choices: Buy a mask and let his family go hungry or buy food and go out into the crowded city without one. Like many poor South Asians, Khan had no choice but to leave the house for work. But with the squeeze on his earnings, his question was, "Should I buy a mask or food for my family?" With basic disposable masks costing up to $7 in some places, it is just another form of inequality in cities where hundreds of millions live in cramped, unhygienic conditions.

Meenakshi Ganguly, South Asia director for Human Rights Watch, said the coronavirus lockdown measures had disproportionately hurt marginalised communities. "Certainly the coronavirus itself does not distinguish between prince or pauper, race or religion," Ganguly said. "But how it impacts individuals differs vastly depending on their access to food, shelter, health and other basic needs." In Sri Lanka, authorities capped prices at 15 rupees (eight cents) for a disposable surgical-style mask and 150 rupees for the closer-fitting ones sometimes called respirators. Yet locals said it was difficult to find either at those prices, with pharmacies marking up costs. "Earlier we bought surgical masks for 15 rupees, but now they are not available at that price and some sell the same masks at 75 rupees," said Hashan, who lives in a slum in the capital Colombo.

Researchers predict a sharp increase in poverty even in the most powerful nations of the world, like the US.[5] "If quarterly unemployment hits 30 per cent—as the president of one Federal Reserve Bank predicts—15.4 per cent of Americans will fall into poverty for the year, the Columbia researchers found, even in the unlikely event the economy instantly recovers."[6] Sarah Halpern-Meekin, a sociologist at the University of Wisconsin, said: "Poverty represents a level of deprivation that many middle- or upper-income Americans can't even wrap their head around… the first thing that come to mind is a mother I met who was trying to manage her son's asthma while living in an apartment that had rodents, insects and mould no matter how much she cleaned. Rising poverty rates means more families living like that."[7] All these economic pointers underline the fact that the coronavirus pandemic is bringing about another pandemic, of poverty, which will perhaps be a serious "humanitarian catastrophe."

David Beasley, the head of the United Nations World Food Programme (UNWFP), has warned that the world is on "the brink of a hunger pandemic" due to the coronavirus. If audacious and apposite actions are not taken rapidly, the world could face "multiple famines of biblical proportions" that "more people could potentially die from the impact of COVID-19 than from the virus itself."[8] As the UN's logistics backbone, Beasley presented an appalling statement of facts on 21 April 2020 at the virtual session of the UN Security Council on the Maintenance of International Peace and Security: Protecting Civilians Affected by Conflict-Induced Hunger:[9]

We are not only facing a global health pandemic but also a global humanitarian catastrophe. Millions of civilians living in conflict-scarred nations, including many women and children, face being pushed to the brink of starvation, with the spectre of famine a very real and dangerous possibility. This sounds truly shocking but let me give you the numbers: 821 million people go to bed hungry every night all over the world, chronically hungry, and as the new Global Report on Food Crisis published today shows, there are a further 135 million people facing crisis levels of hunger or worse. That means 135 million people on earth are marching towards the brink of starvation. But now the World Food Programme analysis shows that, due to the Coronavirus, an additional 130 million people could be pushed to the brink of starvation by the end of 2020. That's a total of 265 million people.

On any given day now, WFP offers a lifeline to nearly 100 million people, up from about 80 million just a few years ago. This includes about 30 million people who literally depend on us to stay alive. If we can't reach these people with the life-saving assistance they need, our analysis shows that 300,000 people could starve to death every single day over a three-month period. This does not include the increase of starvation due to Covid-19. In a worst-case scenario, we could be looking at famine in about three dozen countries, and in fact, in 10 of these countries we already have more than one million people per country who are on the verge of starvation. In many places, this human suffering is the heavy price of conflict.

Caste, Power and Poverty

The coronavirus has been called a great leveller, and to some extent it is true. But in India, as writer-activist Suraj Yengde, the author of *Caste Matters*, says, the coronavirus has "reaffirmed India's caste and class inequalities." The lockdown to check the spread of the novel coronavirus disease sparked a mass "reverse exodus" of migrant labourers. With disturbing images of migrant workers stranded on highways and being sprayed with disinfectants surfacing, many have criticised the state's handling of the situation. Most of the workers were agricultural migrants, Dalits or Adivasis. During the lockdown, several contractual workers were fired and many of them were not eligible for the relief package as they did not have construction worker welfare board cards. This is due to the insensitivity of the authorities who never understood their lives. There is no representation; a vote, after all, does not guarantee representation.

Caste is the oldest form of social exclusion in India, "sanctioned" by religious texts and ritual practices and toughened through "inner-marriages" and "inner-dining." According to World Bank Reports, prepared by Maitreyi Bordia Das and Soumya Kapoor Mehta, education and the labour market have had significant implications for poverty and other welfare outcomes for Dalits in India. "This is because education and occupation both had ritual significance in that they were the preserve of upper castes. Dalits were usually illiterate, landless and were meant to serve in 'impure' occupations passed down through generations."[10]

In the labour market, Dalits largely remain in the unorganised sector because historically Dalits have been landless. In spite of reservation in government jobs, Dalit men still lag behind non-Scheduled Caste/Scheduled Tribe communities in regular salaried work and not many among them who are self-employed graduate from casual labour. Dalits are still slotted into their traditional occupations, which are manual work with low wages. In 2006, almost 60 per cent of the sweepers in Central government ministries were from the Scheduled Caste community. Wage differentials between Dalits and others are a testimony to their continued disadvantage in the labour market which further reinforces horizontal segregation, otherwise known as "glass walls." There are glass ceilings as well, which make it difficult for Dalit workers to obtain high-status, better-paid jobs.

According to World Bank reports, education—considered as a panacea for poor labour market outcomes—appears to disadvantage men in the rural sector. This anomaly shows three things: "First, that all men with education in a rural, primarily agricultural context are penalised; second, that Dalit men feel these effects more if they have post-primary education; and third, that growth of jobs in rural areas has not kept pace with the increase in the supply of educated Dalit men."[11] Caste is an important reason for poverty in India. Despite the visible transformation in the political arena—in the form of movements around Dalit identity and dignity—remnants of the caste system continue to mutate in different ways. It makes the fulfilment of Ambedkar's dream (1936) of annihilating caste in India indefinitely delayed.

Ekklēsia as Community Kitchen

An op-ed for *La Stampa* newspaper (in Italian) on a historic verdict by Italy's highest court on food theft by a young hungry homeless man was titled: "Right to survival prevails over property."[12] In 2011, Roman Ostriakov, who had bought a bag of breadsticks from a supermarket, slipped a packet of sausages (*wurstel*) and two pieces of cheese worth €4.07 into his pocket. Ostriakov, from Ukraine, was sentenced to six months in jail and a €100 fine by a lower court in Genoa. While vacating the punishment of Ostriakov, the supreme court observed that the theft did not constitute a crime as the accused was in desperate need of food.[13] For many humanists, the case draws parallels with the story of Jean Valjean, the hero of Victor Hugo's *Les Misérables*.

Perhaps a more important and larger political initiative to alleviate poverty among migrants is the "community kitchen" in Kerala, India, during the pandemic. It is not a populist measure but a government initiative done in convergence with local governing bodies, Arogya Sena (Health Army) and Kudumbashree (women's empowerment movement) to ensure food security for people on the margins. A state with a robust public food distribution system and an extraordinary record in maintaining standards of public health and literacy, Kerala has also been the most successful in combating the virus. The social kitchens in the state were reminiscent of the soup kitchens in the West during the Depression or the food basket programme (zero hunger programme) in Brazil and elsewhere. Through as many as 1,225 community kitchens, the Kerala state government provided on an average 300,000 food packets a day to daily-wage workers from other states and the homeless during the lockdown.

Community kitchens are an important part of the food security programme for various reasons. In cities, poor people do not have an option but to depend on street food. When there are price hikes (as that of dal (pulses) and of onions earlier in India), the poor are often the hardest hit. Community kitchens can provide relief at such times by offering food at fixed prices. Women are often burdened with providing packed food for working men. If men have the option of a decent meal at such canteens, women get some relief from the daily drudgery. Further, in several states, community kitchens are run and managed by women, providing them an independent source of income. Such kitchens help in the creation of democratic spaces much required in our deeply-divided society.[14]

Diakonia as Politics of Food Protocol

Sharing a meal with people from diverse backgrounds to foster a spirit of togetherness is what diakonia should be in the context of pandemic and poverty. Food is (it should be) an important materiality that constitutes our faith. After creating human beings, God commands them about their food, which is a basic human need. It does show that God is concerned about our food. This is further reinforced in many instances in the Old Testament, for instance, in the story of Joseph, who becomes instrumental in resolving the food crisis of his fellow human beings (Gen 42); the story of Elijah, where God entrusts his food with a widow in Zarephath (1 Kings 17).

According to Gregory Fewster, the story of Joseph (Gen 37–50) unfolds the connection between economic power and the centrality of food. Joseph develops a clear and crude relation between food and power, as evidenced earlier by his relationship to the cupbearer.[15] This is further evident in Joseph's creative solution to the food shortage crisis. He capitalises on the Pharaoh's vulnerability from the threat of a famine, food shortage and starvation. This is where "expert interpreters" of scarcity/famine/pandemic tactfully secure positions in the corridors of power.[16] Joseph advises the Pharaoh to fashion a political economy to organise a monopoly of grain and thus could administer resources for the *subsistence* of agricultural peasants and for the *luxury* of the Pharaoh and his urban/court elites (who managed the state economy for the sake of their surplus).[17] This capacity to administer grain supplies is of course evident in the Bible in the "storehouse cities" of the Pharaoh (Ex 1:11, Gen 47:13-19).

Joseph becomes the caretaker of life and death in the empire as he is in control of the food surplus. The one who controls food production and distribution controls the lives of the people who depend on that food for survival. Clark Cochran observes rightly that Joseph used his control over Egypt's food and that his actions essentially enslaved his people to the Egyptians.[18] During this pandemic, who controls food distribution? If food production and distribution is owned and controlled by the elites, like the "visionary Joseph," who know the art of combining food and power during this pandemic, the post-COVID age in India and elsewhere would be an age of pandemic of poverty and slavery. Diakonia in this age, therefore, means exposing the politics of food and power.

Another significant instance is the manna incident (Ex 16). Upon the delivery of the people of Israel, the wandering Israelites cried for food. God provided his people food even in the wilderness for forty years. This is what the Lord has commanded: "Gather as much of it as each of you needs, an omer to a person according to the number of persons, all providing for those in their own tents. The Israelites did so, some gathering more, some less. But when they measured it with an omer, those who gathered much had nothing over, and those who gathered little had no shortage; they gathered as much as each of them needed." (Ex 16:16-18)

God's provisions of manna and conditions for its consumption and storage is an invitation for counter/covenantal practice and social living. Amassing food is antithetical to God's imagination of a liberated community. It is also a warning not to mimic the Egyptian imperial practice of monopolising earthly or God-given resources for sustenance. The wilderness became a God-initiated community kitchen. Like in the community kitchen, manna was available every day. But manna was given according to need, and not according to their greed (Ex 16: 18). The manna economy of food is based on need.

God's concern for people's food is further reinforced in the New Testament. The miracles of feeding the multitude are wondrous narratives signifying how serious Jesus was about people's hunger: "You give them something to eat." (Mark 6:37) As Brueggemann observes, Jesus treats the "food insecure" with dignity and provides enough that they become "food secure." "The work of abundance is to move the neighbours who are food insecure into the circle of those who are food secure. These acts of abundance do not make everyone equal. But they do open the prospect for the abundant life."[19]

During these miracles too, as in Exodus 16, the wilderness becomes a social kitchen. Jesus reiterates the wonder of the manna bread in the wilderness after feeding the crowd (John 6). The abundance was so great that twelve baskets of bread were left over from his lordly act. After the miracle, Jesus asked his disciples to collect the leftover bread and fish (Mark 6: 43). This is not to cater to the unnecessary fear of loss and overvalue new things ("overestimated scarcity" or "imagined scarcity"), unlike in the parable of the rich fool in Luke 12:13-21. In Luke, the rich man is suffering from imagined scarcity. Whereas, Jesus invites his followers to celebrate God's abundance, not practice scarcity.[20]

Diakonia in the context of pandemic hunger means practising materiality of food, including critical reflection on food. Reengaging "materiality of faith" is not to be confused with materialism. The material aspect of faith is grounded in the theological conviction about the essential goodness of creation (Gen 1-3). It is further grounded in our conviction that

God has become bodied ("became flesh," John 1:14) in Jesus of Nazareth, who "went about doing good" (Acts 10:38) of a vigorously material kind (Luke 7:22). In Brueggemann's view, this has to be implemented at three levels: food production, food distribution and food consumption.[21] This calls for an alternative identity—identity as citizens and members of the community, and identity as creatures of God. Such personal reidentification alters our self-understanding as consumers. Mary the mother of Jesus invites all of us to embrace the diaconal practice of radical distribution of food. "He has filled the hungry with good things, and sent the rich away empty" (Luke 1:53). If diakonia means radical redistribution of food, then ekklēsia evolves into an inclusive table fellowship, trusting in God's assurances against food scarcity.

Conclusion

Food scarcity was assumed to be "normal" before the pandemic. What would it be in the age of the "new normal"? Would the faith community (ekklēsia) regard the coexistence of "the food secure" and "the food insecure" in its neighbourhood or elsewhere as "normal" in the post-COVID age as well? As Brueggemann points out: "It turns out that 'scarcity' is not a given in the world. It is, rather, a construct proposed by those who do not want to share, who would rather have the 'food insecure' as enemies rather than neighbours." COVID-19 further problematises the givenness of scarcity. In a context such as this pandemic, diakonia means practising eucharistic food protocols and alternative politics of food security. It is through the diakonia of practising God's abundance which subverts our normalised scarcity that ekklēsia happens/evolves as a community of the "food secure." This is the liturgical wonder that the faith community practises and celebrates in and through the "wonder of bread" called the Eucharist.

The diaconal vocation of the faith community is to build grassroots local food systems based on agroecological food production that can outperform the prevailing industrial food systems. As a model of agriculture, agroecology is based on traditional knowledge and modern agricultural research, utilising elements of contemporary ecology, soil biology and the biological control of pests. Decentralised, local community-owned food systems based on shorter food-supply chains that can cope with future shocks are now needed more than ever. In this regard the "Arakunomics model" of the Naandi Foundation, a Hyderabad-based non-profit organisation, in regions of Araku, Wardha, and New Delhi is an apt example. It was selected as one of the top 10 visionaries in the world for the Food System Vision 2050 Prize by the Rockefeller Foundation, announced in New York on 6 August 2020. The Arakunomics model follows an "ABCDEFGH" framework that is centred on agriculture, biology, compost, decentralised decision-making, entrepreneurs, families, global markets and "headstands" (implying innovation). This "food-print" may be considered a potential model of diakonia in the context of the pandemic-induced poverty. It could transform faith communities in to agroeco*klēsia* (agro-eco-*ekklēsia*).

Endnotes

[1] https://www.bbc.com/news/business-52103666 (31 March 2020).

[2] http://whatsaup.in/world-bank-chief-warns-extreme-poverty-could-surge-by-100-million/ (21 August 2020).

[3] https://timesofindia.indiatimes.com/videos/city/jaipur/shocking-starving-man-ends-up-eating-a-dead-dog-in-jaipur/videoshow/75864167.cms; https://www.theweek.in/news/india/2020/05/22/video-of-starving-man-eating-dog-carcass-in-rajasthan-causes-outrage.html

⁴ https://www.ndtv.com/india-news/coronavirus-video-shows-migrants-fighting-over-packet-of-food-at-bihar-train-station-2228706

⁵ Zachary Parolin and Christopher Wimer, "Forecasting Estimates of Poverty During the Covid-19crisis," *Poverty and Social Policy Brief*, Vol. 4/6 (16 April 2020): 1–18.

⁶ Jason DeParle, "A Gloomy Prediction on How Much Poverty Could Rise," (16 April 2020). https://www.nytimes.com/2020/04/16/upshot/coronavirus-prediction-rise-poverty.html

⁷ Jason DeParle, "A Gloomy Prediction on How Much Poverty Could Rise," (16 April 2020). https://www.nytimes.com/2020/04/16/upshot/coronavirus-prediction-rise-poverty.html

⁸ https://www.wfp.org/news/wfp-chief-warns-hunger-pandemic-covid-19-spreads-statement-un-security-council (21 April 2020).

⁹ https://www.wfp.org/news/wfp-chief-warns-hunger-pandemic-covid-19-spreads-statement-un-security-council (21 April 2020).

¹⁰ Maitreyi Bordia Das and Soumya Kapoor Mehta, "Poverty and Social Exclusion in India," (21 April 2020). https://openknowledge.worldbank.org/bitstream/handle/10986/26336/114155-BRI-India-PSE-Dalits-Brief-PUBLIC.pdf?sequence=1&isAllowed=y

¹¹ Maitreyi Bordia Das and Soumya Kapoor Mehta, "Poverty and Social Exclusion in India," (21 April 2020). https://openknowledge.worldbank.org/bitstream/handle/10986/26336/114155-BRI-India-PSE-Dalits-Brief-PUBLIC.pdf?sequence=1&isAllowed=y

¹² Massimo Gramellini, "The right to be hungry," 3 May 2020). https://www.lastampa.it/opinioni/buongiorno/2016/05/03/news/il-diritto-di-avere-fame-1.34996997

¹³ Stephanie Kirchgaessner, "Theft of sausage and cheese by hungry homeless man 'not a crime,'" (3 May 2020). https://www.theguardian.com/world/2016/may/03/theft-sausage-cheese-hungry-homeless-man-not-crime-italy

¹⁴ Reetika Khera, "Community kitchens: An idea whose time has come," (22 June 2020). https://scroll.in/article/801742/community-kitchens-an-idea-whose-time-has-come

¹⁵ Gregory P. Fewster, "Food, Power, and Ecological Hermeneutics: Reading Joseph with Monsanto," in *Reading Bible in the Age of Political Crisis* (Bruce Worthington, ed., Minneapolis: Fortress, 2015): 191–211.

[16] James C. Scott, *Against the Grain: A Deep History of the Earliest States* (New Haven and London: Yale University Press, 2017).

[17] Roland Boer, *The Sacred Economy of Ancient Israel* (Louisville, Kentucky: John Knox Press, 2015)

[18] Fewster, "Food, Power, and Ecological Hermeneutics," 210-11.

[19] Walter Brueggemann, "There is no Excuse for Food Security," (15 July 2020).https://churchanew.org/blog/posts/walter-brueggemann-column-theres-no-excuse-for-food-insecurity?fbclid=IwAR2kKgfI_nZ-MBZiN74uPXip6iHqXGG80GnOXc-eErUofG_xD0DstnI6WWo

[20] Brueggemann, *Materiality as Resistance: Five Elements for Moral Action in the Real World* (Louisville, Kentucky: John Knox Press, 2020), Kindle Location 420.

[21] Brueggemann, *Materiality as Resistance*, Kindle Location 440ff.

Chapter 7

Rethinking Ekklēsia and Pastoral Care in the Age of COVID-19

While many of the businesses that have stayed open, or are being authorized to reopen, are inherently transactional, what happens in churches is inherently social and relational. We eat together; we sing together; we embrace one another; we care for one another's children. These familiar patterns have been ingrained in us through years of meeting together, and will be challenging for many to shake even when we know the risk and have a plan in place.

Kent Annan and Jamie D. Aten

It is the task and glory of the church to inhabit and to bear witness to Covenantal time that frontally contradicts the Promethean time by which most of us reckon our days. The church does that by slo-time liturgy (even if on-line for now), by serious engagement with the vulnerable, by the wonder of baptism whereby we are named persons and not "data," and by the great festival of abundance in the Eucharist that contradicts the passionate scarcity of Promethean time, as in "I don't have enough time!

Walter Brueggemann

Introduction

Manjhi – The Mountain Man (2015) is a Hindi-language movie based on the life of Dashrath Manjhi. Manjhi was a labourer in Gehlaur village near Gaya in Bihar, India. He earned the sobriquet "The Mountain Man" for carving a path 9.1 metres (30 ft) wide and 110 metres (360 ft) long through a hill 7.6 metres (25 ft) high using only a hammer and a chisel. *The Mountain Man* ends with a pertinent statement from Manjhi, played by Nawazuddin Siddiqui, "Don't wait for God to act; God may be placing his hope in us." As the number of coronavirus infections surge in the country, the faith community is called to diaconally and compassionately act/intervene/intercede to discover new forms of "deep solidarity" with the victims and the marginalised, rather than waiting for God to act in mysterious and supernatural ways, and thus become an ekklēsia of God. Ekklēsia is not "a nag or a nanny" but a resilient community bearing witness to the "normals that are ordained of God and structured into the creation that cannot for long be outflanked or violated with impunity."[1]

In the midst of the coronavirus-induced "new normal," God has called us out to be a covenantal community (ekklēsia) with a prophetic voice of dissent through covenantal social practices (diakonia) of being the salt and the light of the earth. To be God's ekklēsia is a calling into the public square to be in diaconal solidarity with the voices of dispute, dissent, protest and advocacy on the streets and the margins. The "dangerous oddness" of ekklēsia is always at odds with the destructive abnormalities of the pre/post-COVID world, which have been recast as normal. More important, God's ekklēsia challenges "the perpetrators of phony normals" and capitalistic totalism, which is completely impatient with and intolerant of any alternative or counter-thinking; it is legitimated by an "anaemic God," whose only function is to bless it. In this intersectional sense, ekklēsia negotiates the non-negotiable agapeic justice of God through prophetic diakonia and inclusive pastoral care.

Ekklēsia in the Age of COVID-19

Since the pandemic struck, leaving large parts of the world in various stages of lockdown, there have been several calls for solidarity. Various Christian faith communities have reimagined new diaconal ways of being an ekklēsia of God. These communities have tried to be true to the values of humanism and the "kingdom of God" by offering their material resources and premises, such as auditoriums and schools, to be converted into quarantine centres or hospitals. Pastors have also reimagined their vocation in contextually relevant ways that could facilitate combating COVID-19, strengthening patients and their family members and ensuring a dignified burial for those who succumbed to the virus.

In Mumbai, a number of religious institutions—churches and Jain temples—opened their doors for coronavirus patients. In Mahim, the St. Michael's Church, the oldest Franciscan Church in Mumbai, built by the Portuguese in 1534, showed that only one creed matters in the battle against COVID-19: "Scale the barriers, blur the lines, come together." Shut since the beginning of the lockdown, the church readily offered its premises to be turned into a healthcare centre and as an isolation facility for nurses from the Hinduja Hospital in Mumbai. The decision was taken after the Brihanmumbai Municipal Corporation (BMC) requested the church to do so owing to its proximity to the hospital.

With Mizoram facing shortage of quarantine facilities, 168 churches in the state from various denominations, such as the Presbyterian Church, the Baptist Church of Mizoram (BCM), the Salvation Army (SA), the Lairam Isua Krista Baptist Kohhran (LIKBK), the Evangelical Church of Maraland (ECM), the United Pentecostal Church (NEI) and the United Pentecostal Church (Mizoram), offered their premises to be used as quarantine facilities. Chief Minister Zoramthanga tweeted: "And with the Churches strengthening their various spiritual and physical supports towards curbing this COVID-19 pandemic, Mizoram just got restored again to one powerhouse of Love Peace and Unity."

With confusion prevailing about safety, non-availability of undertakers and an inability to dig graves 10 feet deep as per government norms, Sahrida, the social service arm of the Ernakulam-Angamaly Archdiocese of the Kerala-based Syro-Malabar Church, formed a special burial squad to assist in funerals during the pandemic. The group, called "Sahridaya Samaritans," including priests and young volunteers trained under the leadership of government health workers to handle bodies as per COVID-19 protocols, ensured proper burials to all Catholics dying of coronavirus without unnecessary fear and doubt.

Bushels of paddy carpeted a community hall that usually hosts wedding feasts because a church in Kerala opened its doors to farmers to dry their harvest, delayed due to the pandemic. The church came to the rescue of farmers in a village in Thrissur, the cultural capital of the state, as they were staring at the possibility of their harvest from over 40 acres of paddy fields being destroyed by rain-induced moisture. Had the farmers been unable to dry their crop, the grain would have sprouted and mills would not have bought the produce. The paddy would normally have been harvested in mid-May, almost a fortnight before the monsoon arrives in Kerala. But this time, with the virus-related lockdown affecting interstate movement, many labourers who operate the harvesting machines could not reach the state from neighbouring Tamil Nadu.

Reimagining Pastoral Care

According to Laurie Brock, "Remember, the clergy collar does not make you a priest. If you aren't enough without the collar, you'll never be enough with it." Pastoral care is not an ontologically privileged and exclusive function attached to any office, but a shared calling (ekklēsia) and a democratic solidarity (diakonia) of a community rooted in inclusive love as embodied in the person of Jesus, his life and his death on the cross. And, as an office, pastorate is (only) a visible and symbolic embodiment of this collective responsibility. What a pastor performs in and for the community as part of ministerial obligations or how a pastor ministers to people in need is not an impossible task that only a person in a robe can carry out. Instead, the ministry (diakonia) of a pastor is a constant reminder to the community (ekklēsia) itself as to what its members are "called out" for (diakonia). In other words, the care which pastors render to the people is symbolic of the pastoral responsibility and missional identity of the entire ekklēsia.

At a time of extraordinary confusion, uncertainty, panic and loss of control caused by COVID-19, as a deacon signifying the inclusive diaconate of ekklēsia, a pastor has the responsibility to make people look through the critical lens of this devastation to understand what believing in Jesus and following him means.

It looks for authentic ways to live in the repressive conditions of the pandemic and to make the most sense of the world. As Brueggemann says, the virus may be understood as a "summons" to reinvent pastoral care. Like the prophets of the Hebrew Bible, pastors must hear the summons in the midst of disasters and pandemics. This is not a palliative enterprise passively accepting the current calamity, but a summons to preach the injustices and unsustainability of the capitalist neoliberal order that oppresses people—a reality the virus has revealed. Radical neighbourliness, generosity and hospitality are the basis of pastoral care and action in the face of the pandemic.

So pastoral care is "prophetic imagination" and relentless solidarity, giving birth to a new inclusive future to "recontextualize the disasters." This is primarily done by re/positioning invaluable re/sources of pastoral care and ministry, such as the Bible, prayer and liturgy, in a milieu of loss, grief, pain and fear. It is a groan of faith for everyone, including those who minister in difficult situations. If so, what does it mean to say at this time of coronavirus that God is in control of history, nothing is impossible with God, God is loving and caring, God is just and God of Jesus is the healer of the sick?

'Phantom Plague' and Rash Providentialism

Not surprisingly, COVID-19 became a hot-button topic in the culture war among various Christian groups and leaders across the world. Nearly 90 per cent of the congregations closed their churches as per the stay-at-home guidelines of the authorities concerned and are watching live-streamed services. But some popular pastors and televangelists have played down the pandemic and encouraged the members of their respective communities to flout social distancing guidelines and public health warnings. According to the Centers for Disease Control and Prevention (CDC) reports, worship gatherings and religious meetings can be deadly vectors for the disease.[2] President Trump asked governors to reopen churches and worship places as "essential services."[3]

For some leaders, the community of the faithful is immune to the pandemic as though it is a judgement on sinners and the sinful world. American televangelist Kenneth Copeland contends that the people of God have dominion and authority over the virus because Jesus saved people from sickness and plague. He summoned the "wind of God" to destroy the pandemic. An influential Israeli Sephardic Rabbi, Meir Mazuz, said that the coronavirus was a judgement on gay pride parades: "A parade against nature, and when someone goes against nature, the one who created nature takes revenge on him."[4] Israeli Health Minister Yaakov Litzman, also the head of Orthodox Israeli political party Agudat Yisrael, said that all LGBTQ+ people are sinners and that the coronavirus was a "divine punishment for homosexuality." Litzman and his wife later tested positive for COVID-19. In a similar vein, ultraconservative Swiss bishop Eleganti also claimed that the coronavirus was "God's punishment."[5]

Attitudes like this are dangerous to the community. Pastoral approach to COVID-19 cannot be that of deadly providentialism.[6] All historical events are foreordained and hence everything is safe in God's hands. But in times such as this, blatant rejection of scientific temper and common sense could be fatal. It is the height of irresponsibility and performative piety. Rash providentialism is ludicrous as it does not fit into the history of the fate of the early martyred Christians. French bishop Raymond Centène, of Vannes in Brittany, ripped reckless providentialists and said they were "tempting God" during a pandemic as "the host remains subject to the laws of nature." The bishop recalled the heroic examples of fearless saints: "Their witness was at the cost of their own lives and not at the risk of the health and life of their neighbour."[7]

As much as relevant pastoral care means not giving in to widespread fearmongering, it is also about understanding the psychological aspect of fear and not hiding human fragility. It also encourages people to see disasters as occasions to experience divine grace through neighbourliness. Practising neighbourly solidarity defies any attempt to attach cause-effect logic to the crisis. And this is "raw holiness," as Brueggemann rightly defines it, one that does not reduce God's force to any material reality.[8] This would provide a persuasive premise for pastors who face the issue of theodicy amidst the pandemic.

Praying Amid the Virus

An important function of pastoral care in this time is to relocate COVID-19 to a covenantal relationship with God. And this is realised primarily through prayer. Through prayer we grow in realising God's ontological solidarity with creation and thus it embodies/enacts a trusting relationship. In his recent book, *Virus as a Summons to Faith: Biblical Reflections in a Time of Loss, Grief, and Uncertainty*, Brueggemann outlines an interface between pestilence and prayer. This is an important resource for pastors elucidating the power of prayer during a pandemic that reminds us about the inadequacy of the autonomous self. Referring to 1 Kings 8: 23-53, a prayer of Solomon at the dedication of the Jerusalem temple, Brueggemann suggests that "prayer is the effective antidote for every form of disaster... however...

antidote is in the form of trust and not a flat certitude."[9] In a context such as a pandemic, when people look for answers, solutions and certainty through prayer, the goal of pastoral care is to recontextualise the pandemic through prayer in such a way that it becomes epiphanic occasions for renewing faith and reinvigorating covenantal life.

'Dying for Dummies': Ecology of Death

In the face of a terrible global pandemic, one of the challenging responsibilities of a pastor is to help people accept the frightening possibility of death without fear and despair. It is possible that anybody could be infected and severe illness and death could follow. People do get morbidly preoccupied with the fear of death and how a pandemic could destroy their life and world. In the case of COVID-19 or a similar outbreak, having a priest present to prepare for the inevitable could be difficult. The ecology of the natural world is the key to the ecology of death. Death is not an enemy as it constitutes the ecology of the natural order of creation. But there is a more profound response possible, which looks forward to a Christian hope that is available to the ekklēsia through the resurrection of Jesus.

Preaching and embodying a radical and subversive hope amidst this coronavirus pandemic is what people expect through pastoral care and ministry. We have witnessed some consummate examples of such pastoral ministry during this crisis. There are reports that Don Giuseppe Berardelli, 72, an Archpriest in Casnigo, Italy, died of COVID. He chose to put others' lives before his own by giving his breathing apparatus to save the life of a young person at the same hospital.[10] Berardelli's gesture of "vulnerable generosity" does not jeopardise the sanctity of life but is a powerful manifestation of hope over death. More importantly, Berardelli proves that the value of life means making one's life valuable for others and embracing death with a sense of fullness and completion, as Jesus died on the cross saying, "It is finished." This is a message of hope and courage to those dying with severe breathing illness that they can avoid ending their earthly voyage unfinished.

Furthermore, it accentuates the sacramentality of the present time—presentness or nowness. Each moment in life is a completion by itself. Even in the minutiae of life, God's work is fulfilled (Rom 8:28). Numbness is the sign of the times. But nowness is creative celebration of time and it positions itself in the ecology of time and space. This is not simply accepting and endorsing all evil realities in time. It is a an "abandonment to divine providence," as the title of a book by eighteenth century French Catholic spiritual director Jean Pierre de Caussade argues. Pastoral care attempts to help people to live life to its fullest in each moment and complete one's relationships on earth.

Following the standard operating procedure (SOP) on COVID deaths is even more painful as the guidelines deprive the family of the bereaved a final goodbye. Ignorance and irrational fears of people make funerals more damaging to family members. In many countries, the family do not even receive the body. The news about the bodies of patients being "dumped" worsen the grief of loss. As a representative of the royal priesthood of the ekklēsia, pastors have a diaconal role in making an awful experience into a beautiful memory not only by organising online memorials but also by equipping the family to comfort coronavirus-affected people.

Mourning as a Pastoral Act

In the face of the pandemic, mourning signifies authentic pastoral care and prophetic intervention. It is a radical response to many corona-induced questions about Christianity and Christian faith. Pastors are vulnerable and mortal human beings like the people they minister to. Neither them nor the faith they profess offers any answers or explanations regarding the coronavirus nor are they supposed to indulge in dodgy speculations. In this respect, mourning is a confessional declaration of human fragility and the intellectual helplessness of the pastor. Lamenting is what pastors do (or are supposed to do) when people cry out for help and hope and ask, "Why?" In the process of mourning, pastors invite the tortured ones to "wait without hope," borrowing what T.S. Eliot said. It is not pessimism because it is better not to define or qualify our hope for what if we would be hoping for the wrong thing?[11]

What makes lamenting a pastoral and a prophetic act at the same time? By mourning, the community of faithful move beyond understanding their self-centred worries through the logic of cause-effect or sin-punishment and look at the afflictions of the world in a much broader perspective. As a result, ekklēsia is able to lament larger political sufferings such as issues in Gaza, South Sudan, Syria and Myanmar. Lamenting is more than an outlet for expressing loneliness, regret and human inability. In fact, the liturgical act of lamenting is a sacramental act because the ekklēsia is not lamenting alone or for/by itself but participating with the lament of the spirit within us. St. Paul speaks of the spirit "groaning" within us. That is, mourning is not a passive act of empathy but a radical liturgical invention that can open up new imaginations of kindness and solidarity.

Through liturgical lamenting, pastors invite the community of the faithful to reimagine itself as an inclusive fellowship of the "faceless and anonymous." The images of bodies stacked in Italy, of an ice rink in Madrid converted into a temporary morgue, of body bags piling up in nursing homes in New Jersey all tell stories of how the bodies of the dead become a logistical problem. Lamenting mass death means valuing the life of each and every person, irrespective of ethnic, linguistic and religious boundaries. Nor do we have to know the person or to visit a country or a community to mourn. In Judith Butler's views, and rightly so, "All these lost lives are grievable, which means that they are lives worthy of acknowledgment, equal in value to every other life, a value that cannot be calculated."[12] What someone else suffers is not one's own suffering, but the loss that the stranger endures traverses the personal loss one feels, potentially connecting strangers in grief. Pain connects peoples and communities, even those who live at an unbridgeable distance. The act of lamenting, thus, sets a new liturgical premise for radical solidarity.

The liturgical act of mourning is woven into the fabric of biblical tradition—God also laments. The book of Genesis declares that God grieved in his heart seeing the wickedness on earth. The book of Exodus records how God lamented at the plight of his people (Exo 2:23). It leads to divine intervention in the life of the suffering people. Brueggemann observes: "Exodus narrative does not begin—as Calvinists are wont to say—with divine initiative. It begins rather with Israel 'groaning and crying out' in the burden of oppression that has become unbearable for the slaves."[13]Lamenting in this sense is epiphanic as it precedes liberation. God responds to the mourning of his people. This is well reflected in Psalms (Psalms 13, 22, 89). Jesus himself cited Psalms 22 during his excruciating agony on the cross. Jesus wept at the tomb of his friend Lazarus. Lamenting is a very vital act of pastoral care in the context of the pandemic as it participates in God's lament for his people, which leads to theophanic intervention.

Alternative Ways of Pastoral Care

Any serious crisis is a summons to reread the Bible, which is the primary source of faith. Making sense of the Bible and faith in context through preaching is an important task of pastoral care. Conventional pulpits and biblical interpretations may not make any sense in the context of disease distancing, poverty and panic. The coronavirus pandemic is a wake-up call for pastors to reinvent pastoral care through innovative ways of preaching the gospel.

Kitchen as Pulpit: Warner D'Souza, a 50-year-old Catholic priest and pastor of Mumbai's St. Jude's Church, is also a professionally-trained chef. He converted his kitchen into his pulpit, preaching from his kitchen at home in a suburb of North Mumbai, across a counter laden with garden-fresh vegetables and finely ground spices for a one-pot meal. D'Souza gives a homily prior to his YouTube programme, "Food for the Soul", a series of lockdown lessons about food and spirituality. D'Souza was inspired to start his new medium of preaching when a news story cited food as the most intense issue in everyone's life since the lockdown was announced. He said, "I felt the pulpit could be the church or the kitchen.... The stereotype of a priest in a white cassock with bent knees takes away the humanness of a person.... From baking bread that satisfies human hunger, I turned to breaking bread to fulfil people's spiritual needs."[14] D'Souza makes the pulpit palatable to people in need.

The Bed of the Sick as Altar: One example of brave clerics on the frontlines against coronavirus is Italian priest Father Alberto Debbi, who decided to exchange his cassock for the doctor's gown. Father Debbi temporarily left his church to resume his duties as a doctor and thus help his former colleagues at the Sassuolo hospital in the province of Modena, Italy, during the COVID crisis. "My altar will be the bed of the sick," said the 43-year-old who trained as a lung doctor and practised for twelve years before entering the seminary in 2013. In this way, Father Debbi once again practised his specialty, pulmonology, during the pandemic. "There is a need, right now like never before, to make everything you have available. I am a doctor specialised in the branch of which now has a particular need and I certainly cannot back down," explained the priest.

But pastoral ministry is both a vocation and a calling, not a responsibility or a privilege principally confined to the ecclesiastical offices of the clergy. All members of the faith community, by virtue of their baptism, share a common priesthood (1 Peter 2:9). In this respect, like Father Debby, Dr. Keerthana Rajkumar, a young doctor from Christian Medical College (CMC), Vellore, has been doing a genuine ministry of pastoral care to COVID patients. Until diagnosed positive, Keerthana regarded only her COVID patients' beds in CMC as altars to offer her life and healthcare skills. But personal experience as a patient with coronavirus made her to accept her own body as an altar, not just her patient's beds. It altered her perspective on healthcare and fundamentally transformed the way she practices medicine. She is a wounded healer now, subjectively understanding the volatile physical and emotional trail that COVID patients go through. Last heard, she was looking forward to donate her plasma to help save critically-ill patients. Keerthana is definitely an alternative example of pastoral care the faith community must celebrate and embrace at least in the age of COVID-19.

Worship on Wheels (WOW): Worship in the Time of Pandemic: Extraordinary situations demand extraordinary imagination and innovation. This is true of effective pastoral care. Being representative facilitators of corporate worship, pastors are expected to minister to people suffering. Due to social distancing and other protocols for preventive measures, formal worship gathering becomes impossible. The Bible clearly assures the ekklēsia about God's presence in the midst of his people irrespective of the historical situations and spatial constraints. (Matt 18:20). This calls for innovative forms of worship compatible with WHO guidelines.

Following the method of "Worship of Wheels" (WOW) in the Philippines, which has food programmes, disaster relief and children's ministry, the Bengaluru Assemblies of God (AG) church also started the concept of "Worship on Wheels" in Hebbal, India.[15] It is aimed at "safe, contactless, drive-in-worship." Worshippers park outside in their cars, roll down the windows and worship from inside their vehicles while the pastor leads the service from the dais, which is telecast on multiple screens outside. They have also made thermal scanning and masks compulsory, provided sanitisers and distributed items for the Holy Communion in pre-packaged sets. Leaving our valid criticisms aside about it being exclusive, "Worship on Wheel" challenges ministers to reimagine pastoral care (diakonia) to make a moving ekklēsia possible, "Church on Wheels."

Virus as Penultimate, not the Ultimate, Threat of Death: Hope and Pastoral care

The upshot of the coronavirus is not foreordained. It is a conflict (forever?), full of the best and the worst possibilities. People of faith obviously turn to pastors for words of hope in the midst of lethal catastrophes. Nuancing the Christian hope that people look for is an important aspect of pastoral care. Hope is not a passive optimism or a civic assurance that everything will be fine, but exploring how people can live through (and live with) the coronavirus to make the most sense of the world and transform the predicament into working towards a more inclusive future. But the enduring basis of such a liberative hope is the understanding of a merciful God in "tenacious solidarity" with humankind in the face of the pandemic. By his/her goodness, God will outflank the fatal force of the virus (Heb 11:1). Brueggemann argues that through this ministry of uncompromising hope, pastors recontextualise the virus as penultimate because God's goodness outflanks even the lethal force of the virus.[16] The diakonia of the pastor is grounded in this hope of the "abiding *ḥesed*" of a God that lingers amid pestilence. This hope is not spectatorial but participatory, argues Cornel West.[17] Hope is a participatory act of courage and imagination. In this sense, hope is a diaconal praxis and the ekklēsia that evolves from such a practice becomes a community of collective hope that exceeds rational and evidence-based optimism.

Digital Pastors and 'No-touch' Ekklēsia

We are in what Arundhati Roy judiciously called the "era of touchlessness, in which the very bodies of one class are seen as a biohazard to another."[18] Human beings are embodied beings; they experience reality through bodily interactions and involvements. But WHO protocol insists on corporeal distancing and self-isolation. Ekklēsia is more than a physical gathering; it happens when love, as manifested in Jesus, is shared and celebrated. Mutually-assured distancing is a gesture of love for the neighbour. In this respect, even in disease, God is present in the midst of people through the Holy Spirit (Matt 18:20; 28:1–20): "He will be there not as a person to touch, but as the bond of love and solidarity between people—so, 'do not touch me, touch and deal with other people in the spirit of love.'"[19] Effective pastoral care is entrusting the community in this spirit of love. Experiencing presence escapes sensory feelings. If experiencing Jesus is possible without touching him (John 20:19), then it should be equally possible to experience the other without touching them.

More importantly, the "pandemic apartheid" (social/physical distancing) provides a historical opportunity to problematise and interrogate the centuries-old caste and race prejudices and their religious groundings. If we are all inter-beings because we constitute the being of the other, and there is no outright divide between embodied and disembodied existence, then doing pastoral care (diakonia) and being ekklēsia during the pandemic is possible only through self-*un*touchability. Social/physical '*un*touchability' is the new definition for community and communion in the so-called "new normal." Pastoral care through church distancing calls for a new ekklēsia that transgresses all mutations of social distancing and untouchability. It is not caste, race or colour that creates untouchability and biohazardous bodies but a virus. Viral untouchability mocks social untouchability; coronavirus taunts the caste/race virus. The coronavirus is challenging us to hermetically seal off the "socially touchable" from the ontologically untouchable. The virus summons both pastors and the ekklēsia to touch and care for the other by not touching the other.

'Dharavi Miracle': Model Ekklēsia in the Age of COVID-19?

The city of Mumbai was a viral hotspot in India. A populace of 12.4 million, always on the move and living in overcrowded conditions, is easy pickings for the raging virus. But, in Mumbai is a place that takes up one-square mile of the city where the pandemic seemed most dreadful. This place is Dharavi. It is one of world's most densely populated areas (with 360,000 people/ square km). Families consisting of those who survive on daily wages sleep in eight-foot-by-eight rooms. Toilets are shared between families. Social distancing, a basic measure in curbing the pandemic, remains almost impossible in Asia's largest slum, the backdrop to the Oscar-winning film *Slumdog Millionaire*.

A 56-year-old garment shop owner was Dharavi's first case of COVID-19 on 1 April 2020. He died the same day. A surgeon working in Wockhardt Hospital was Dharavi's second case. Later his wife too tested positive. Dharavi's infection rate increased frighteningly after that. Home quarantine in matchbox-type homes seemed an unfeasible option. But that did not deter the people here determined to fight the virus. They created 3,000 quarantine beds at a sports complex, a nature park, schools, marriage halls, hotels and guest houses. Once ready, 66 per cent of the infected were quarantined in these facilities. With reports of the virus spreading from common toilets, citizens and sanitary workers sanitised these potential sources at regular intervals. Dharavi's local population, with selfless intervention and the dedicated involvement of healthcare providers and civic authorities, succeeded in flattening the COVID curve.

The "Dharavi Miracle" did not tell the world about complicated treatment modalities or novel preventive strategies. No cry for a vaccine was heard from within Dharavi. No unsubstantiated science, half-truths or scary medical studies were entertained by citizens who were manual labourers living in overcrowded dwellings. The Dharavi miracle told the world that, having come thus far in the global fight against a viral pandemic, the basics remain the cornerstone. That is exactly why WHO Director General Tedros Ghebreyesus, in a virtual press conference on 17 June 2020, praised Dharavi for the efforts of the people to contain the virus in a virtual press conference on 17 June 2020: "There are many examples from around the world that have shown that even if the outbreak is very intense, it can still be brought back under control.... And some of these examples are Italy, Spain and South Korea, and even in Dharavi—a densely packed area in the megacity of Mumbai—a strong focus on community engagement and the basics of testing, tracing, isolating and treating all those that are sick is key to breaking the chains of transmission and suppressing the virus."

While being a society on "the periphery of consciousness" and the government, the people of Dharavi determinedly defied the stereotypical descriptions and ontological comparisons about them through their inclusive solidarity, collective imagination and participation in an informal economy. The Dharavi model of sociability and partnership indicate that the advocacy of people combined with responsible political bodies is definitely a potential option for persistence in the age of COVID. Faith communities have a lot to learn from the Dharavi miracle about the politics of neighbourliness and the spirituality of friendliness. It is through the prophetic facilitation of the collective agency of the people on the margins that the faith community participates and fulfils its diaconal responsibility and covenantal vocation and epiphanically erupts into an ekklēsia of God.

Conclusion

As the WHO Director General rightly said, "This virus thrives when we're divided. When we're united, we can defeat it." Through the spirit of love, a community of faith is present in one another. The other is not opposed to us, but within us. Each person is thus an "inter-being." It particularly helps the ekklēsia in the context of a pandemic to transcend the divide in terms of the embodied and the disembodied. "We are members one another with those we have never met through time and now through space."[20] God is therefore present in a virtual gathering too as God is present in the pain and the sufferings of the cross. In this respect, ekklēsia is both physical and virtual at the same time; people who constitute the ekklēsia must think creatively about "the new permutations of digital and virtual technology informing our lives as particular ways we are embodied."[21] This is important for pastoral care as we are all cyborgs—our bodies are coextensive with nature, and technology.[22] When digital is the new normal and community and communion are more important than physical gathering in extraordinary situations, pastoral care becomes digital attentiveness and digital care.

Endnotes

[1] Walter Brueggemann, "When God's Normal Becomes Abnormal," (24 June 2020). https://churchanew.org/brueggemann/walter-brueggemann-column-when-gods-normal-becomes-abnormal

[2] https://www.cdc.gov/mmwr/volumes/69/wr/mm6915e1.htm?s_cid=mm6915e1_w (17 April 2020).

[3] Gordon Lubold and Catherine Lucey, (22 May 2020). https://www.wsj.com/articles/trump-calls-places-of-worship-essential-11590172336

⁴ https://www.timesofisrael.com/israeli-rabbi-blames-coronavirus-outbreak-on-gay-pride-parades/ (8 March 2020).

⁵ https://novenanews.com/swiss-bishop-served-coronavirus-gods-punishment/ (15 March 2020).

⁶ Rebecca Bratten Weiss, "COVID-19 and Religion: Rash Providentialism Is Going to Get People Killed," (10 March 2020). https://www.patheos.com/blogs/suspendedinherjar/2020/03/providentialism-is-going-to-kill-people/?fbclid=IwAR2UJrfok1GyGKdlsKP9EeIitBJYLu5SGxQM709ZtpbBhunpWs9N0cIQA_k

⁷ https://novenanews.com/bishop-blasts-providentialist-catholics-coronavirus/ (13 March 2020).

⁸ Walter Brueggemann, *Virus as a Summons to Faith: Biblical Reflections in a Time of Loss, Grief, and Uncertainty* (Eugene, Oregon: Cascade Books, 2020), Kindle Edition, location 409.

⁹ Brueggemann, *Virus as a Summons to Faith*, Kindle location, 789.

¹⁰ https://www.cbsnews.com/news/italian-priest-coronavirus-ventilator-don-giuseppe-berardelli/ (24 March 2020).

¹¹ N. T. Wright, "Christianity Offers No Answers About the Coronavirus. It's Not Supposed To," (29 March 2020). https://time.com/5808495/coronavirus-christianity/

¹² George Yancy, "Judith Butler: Mourning Is a Political Act Amid the Pandemic and Its Disparities," (30 April 2020). https://truthout.org/articles/judith-butler-mourning-is-a-political-act-amid-the-pandemic-and-its-disparities/

¹³ Brueggemann, *Virus as a Summons to Faith*, Kindle Edition, 1260.

¹⁴ Priyadarshini Sen, "Making his kitchen his pulpit, Indian priest highlights the pandemic's hungry," (23 March 2020). https://www.ncronline.org/news/coronavirus/making-his-kitchen-his-pulpit-indian-priest-highlights-pandemics-hungry

¹⁵ Ralph Alex Arakal, "As church reopens, a drive-in Mass in Bengaluru parking lot," (15 June 2020). https://indianexpress.com/article/india/church-reopens-bengaluru-parking-lot-drive-in-sunday-mass-6459215/

¹⁶ Brueggemann, *Virus as a Summons to Faith*, Kindle Edition, 721.

¹⁷ Sigal Samuel, Interview with Cornel West, (29 July 2020). https://www.vox.com/futureperfect/2020/7/29/21340730/cornel-west-coronavirus-racism-way-through-podcast?fbclid=IwAR1iddORFIC6pt_4XgNWmYZkBxoi7fs57U4f95766pyNtpPVQ1mk1E3k2eE

[18] Arundhati Roy, "After the lockdown, we need a reckoning," (24 May 2020). https://www.ft.com/content/442546c6-9c10-11ea-adb1-529f96d8a00b

[19] Žižek, *Pandemic*, 1.

[20] Jason Byassee, "For virtual theological education," (2 March 2020). https://faithandleadership.com/jason-byassee-virtual-theological-education

[21] Deanna A. Thompson, "Christ is Really Present Virtually: A Proposal for Virtual Communion," (26 March 2020). (https://wp.stolaf.edu/lutherancenter/2020/03/christ-is-really-present-virtually-a-proposal-for-virtual-communion/?fbclid=IwAR2D8qRuu0yFi18xj_JED1X7uKRwVC_uE1A58W0MogtOaGFpIlRyhEmVt6g. See also Deanna A. Thompson, *The Virtual Body of Christ in a Suffering World* (Nashville, Abingdon: Abingdon Press, 2016)

[22] Lennard Davis, "In the Time of Pandemic, the Deep Structure of Biopower Is Laid Bare," (26 June 2020). https://critinq.wordpress.com/category/2020-pandemic/

Epilogue

As many churches clamour to reenter their buildings, it is worth noting in the book of Acts how infrequently an experience of the Divine takes place in a designed "religious" location. The Holy becomes most strikingly palpable on roads and rooftops, in deserts and prison cells, even through dreams and visions. In our haste to "reopen" our sanctuaries, we may miss the very landscapes of theophany in which the Spirit is manifesting.

Unknown

The crisis will help to remind us, once and for all, that humanity is a single community.... What helps us is synergy, mutual collaboration, the sense of responsibility and the spirit of sacrifice that is generated in many places.... We do not have to make a distinction between believers and nonbelievers; let's go to the root: humanity. Before God, we are all his children.... To remember this difficult experience that we all lived through together and to move forward with hope, which never disappoints. These will be the keywords for starting again: roots, memory, brotherhood and hope.

Pope Francis

In his interview to *The Times of Israel*, Slovenian rock star philosopher Slavoj Žižek made a sharp comment about COVID that literally swamped and rattled the grand apparatus of globalisation. He said after the pandemic the "world as we know it will be just nostalgia."[1] Of course, though celebrities like to say "we are all in this together," everyone does not face the pandemic and the ensuing social disparity in the same way. The so-called "civil society," dominated by the upper middle class, has been able to isolate itself without worrying about future income. The "political society", on the other hand, constituted by the those who are on the margins, has experienced unparalleled hardship, poverty, homelessness and even death. It has created new borders of segregations in cities, towns, streets and even within the space one calls home.[2] Correspondingly, the virus has ostracised many due to the fear of being potential carriers of the virus, leading to a phantasmagoria of panic and anxiety about the pandemic. Acting on this paranoia could result in the death of civility and rationality, as in William Golding's *Lord of the Flies*, where a group of boys trapped on an island during wartime, try to organise themselves to survive but eventually succumb to paranoia.

As we are adjusting and settling into lockdown life, we realise that "normal" was only a delusion. Nick Tilsen, a changemaker who founded the NDN Collective to empower Indigenous people, says: "Everyone says, 'I can't wait until things get back to normal.' There's a part of me that's like, 'Normal never did us justice'.... The normal meant injustices for Indigenous people. The normal meant underinvestment of our people. The normal meant fossil fuel industry exploiting our lands and our communities. This is a point and time for me where we don't want to go back to supporting the same old economic systems and the same old energy systems."[3] This coronavirus-induced rupture is already a reality; we will have to live a more vulnerable life henceforward, convoyed by persistent hazards of the viral contagion. And we will not be able to return to the life we knew as normal. This compels us to find new forms of solidarity and to re/invent ways of life and rituals and imagine the world anew.

With "vaccine nationalism" (governments sign agreements with pharmaceutical manufacturers to supply their own populations with vaccines ahead of them becoming available for other countries in a "go-it-alone approach") increasingly become a concern, the "new normal" is going to be very different, one which no one expected to take shape so quickly. This "go-it-alone approach" would further prolong the coronavirus pandemic.

There have been different definitions for the so-called "new normal". According to Chime Asonye, former senior special assistant on Sustainable Development Goals, World Economic Forum, "The language of a "new normal" is being deployed almost as a way to quell any uncertainty ushered in by the coronavirus."[4] With no cure in sight, everyone from politicians and the media to friends and family has perpetuated this rhetoric as they imagine settling into life under this "new normal." The "new normal" discourse sanitises the idea that our present is okay because normal is regular. The analytic frame embodied by the persistent discussion of the "new normal" helps bring order to our current turbulence, but it should not be the lens through which we examine today's crisis. Far from describing the status quo, evoking the "new normal" does not allow us to deal with the totality of our present reality; "we should use our discomfort to forge a new paradigm instead."

In Jade Begay's view, "prolonged uprising is the new normal."[5] Across the country and the world, people are engaged in civil disobedience, uprising and rebellion. People are coming out to demand justice for the many who have been crushed by injustice, discrimination and violence. If these are our goals, we must get used to and be comfortable with people being in dedicated, committed and prolonged uprising. However, a "prolonged uprising" is not the only thing that is distinctive of the new normal. We also see people caring deeply for each other, observing social distancing protocols, making and distributing masks, organising community kitchens and being involved in awareness programmes.

The crucial question before the faith community in the context of the "new normal," which is hoping to be a gateway between the old world order and the new, is about our diaconal role. Or is God doing to do the impossible for us? If so, it elicits three issues. Why did not God do the same with the old world order? Can we hold God responsible for the failure of the old order and the suffering of the people? Is God responsible for the inequity of deaths mounting from the pandemic? Brueggemann argues that the diaconal praxis of the faith community is to bear witness (witness as diakonia) to the "impossible becoming possible." In so doing, diakonia constitutes an ekklēsia that is "inherently subversive, surprising, and transformative." If diakonia means practising only the conventional imagination of "possibility," then what emerges is an anaemic ekklēsia. What the world reckons to be impossible will be made possible by the "transformative capacity of God." It is to these impossibilities that disrupt the conventional norms of possibilities that the faith community is invited to enter. Entering into these "impossible possibilities" through the "eye of the needle" is what diakonia means in the age of the new normal.[6]

The "new normal" and its potential to make the impossible happen comes up for us in the context of COVID. We have seen that the death of George Floyd and others provide an opportunity to the victims of violence for prophetic solidarity and liberative diakonia to move beyond systemic violence and casteism/racism. In Deenabandhu Manchala's words: "It comes as a warning, but also offers us an opportunity to get rid of all such, and allow ourselves to be transformed into a new people, a new generation with justice, compassion and interdependence as our guiding values, so that all of us are able to breathe—breath freedom, breathe peace, and breathe life."[7] But, not to be forgotten, "the caveat of Gethsemane still persists," says Brueggemann.[8]

The events that unpack the foretaste of the impossible becoming possible in history are *kairos* moments, to use the biblical language. In kairos moments, the foundations of the world shake and the narrative of racism and casteism collapse. It is like a "living soup," as Rebecca Solnit puts it: "In this state, what was a caterpillar and will be a butterfly is neither one nor the other, it's a sort of living soup. Within this living soup are the imaginal cells that will catalyse its transformation into winged maturity."[9] Those who search for God in history might be surprised as such moments shake off false gods who privilege the privileged and demand sacrifice from the less privileged.[10] The challenge before the faith community is to envisage and embrace an alternative response to kairos moments, or "a propitious moment for decision or action" or a time "when things come to a head."[11]

How exactly should the faith community see the coronavirus—as ultimate or penultimate hazard of death? For Brueggemann, and rightly so, it is the "penultimate stage" as even its genocidal mutations are "outflanked by the goodness of God."[12] If George Floyd's pleas to police office Derek Chauvin, who knelt on Floyd's neck and watched him asphyxiate, is an American apocalypse[13] that "unveiled" a whole world of grotesque injustice and centuries-old patterns of terror, then COVID is a global apocalypse as it pulls the mask off of the already existing, and already high, social inequality. COVID is not the end of the world; it is only an apocalypse as it shows the world we think is ending did not really exist. But, what to do with this apocalyptic moment is up to the faith community.

Apocalyptic moments solicit faith communities to be creative collaborators for planetary interdependence. Creative collaboration means that the coming of new creation is a process, and it is participatory. In this process, the collaborators have no control. New creation is not brought into being by a dictator above. Catherine Keller contends: "New creation is not 'top-down' creating. This new creation comes as we cooperate with each other and with the divine source of every other. This is new creativity in and through whatever chaos besets us."[14] In the Bible, *apokalypsis* does not mean the destruction of the physical/material world. "It means *revelation*: not a final closing down, but a great *dis*/closure. 'The new heaven and earth' translate no longer as supernatural intervention or afterlife escape—but as the radical renewal of atmosphere and earth."[15] If COVID-19 is an apocalyptic moment, like the death of Jesus on the cross and the resurrection of the saints, then diakonia means creative collaboration with it and the ekklēsia that thus happens is an eco-spirit cruciform space.

For Christian faith communities, the cross and the resurrection of Jesus is the critical-historical lens through which they capture, caption and capitalise apocalyptic flashes in history such as COVID. This diaconal journalistic activity is both liturgical and political at the same time; liturgical is political and vice versa. Diaconal journalism is a liturgical intercession because it captures disclosures in time and space as subversive divine interventions. Liturgical activity means capturing and collaborating with apocalyptic revelations. It is also a political activity as it facilitates the agency of people through alliance and solidarity. More importantly, like the journalists who seize moments to show a torchlight on the chinks in public space, diakonia captures ekklēsial sparks in history. In other words, by capturing apocalyptic sparks such as the coronavirus, diakonia embodies divine interventions in history; and the ekklēsia that evolves is therefore an archaeological fellowship of the genealogy of such apocalyptic moments.

> *The work of the church is essential.*
> *the work of caring for the lonely, the marginalized,*
> *and the oppressed is essential.*
> *The work of speaking truth to power and*
> *seeking justice is essential.*
> *The work of being a loving, liberating,*
> *and life-giving presence in the world is essential.*
> *The work of welcoming the stranger,*
> *the refugee and the undocumented is essential.*
> *The work of reconciliation and healing*
> *and caring is essential.*
> *The church does not need to "open"*
> *because the church never "closed".*
> *We who make up the Body of Christ, the church,*
> *love God and our neighbours and ourselves so much*
> *that we will stay away from*
> *our buildings until it is safe.*
> *We are the church.*

(Bishop Deon K. Johnson, Episcopal Diocese of Missouri)

Endnotes

[1] Slavoj Žižek, "After pandemic, 'World as we know it will be just nostalgia,'" (20 June 2020). https://www.timesofisrael.com/celeb-philosopher-after-pandemic-world-as-we-know-it-will-be-just-nostalgia/

[2] Vasudeva Naidu K, "The 'alien', the 'self' and the 'other' in times of a pandemic," (17 April 2020). https://countercurrents.org/2020/04/the-alien-the-self-and-the-other-in-times-of-a-pandemic/

[3] Stephanie Petit, How Indigenous People Are Being Affected by Coronavirus — and Why It's Time for a New Normal," (29 April 2020). https://people-com.cdn.ampproject.org/c/s/people.com/human-interest/come-back-stronger-coronavirus-nick-tilsen/?amp=true

[4] https://www.weforum.org/agenda/2020/06/theres-nothing-new-about-this-new-normal-heres-why/ (05 June 2020).

[5] Jade Begay, "Prolonged Uprising Is the New Normal," (15 June 2020). https://www.yesmagazine.org/opinion/2020/06/15/protest-coronavirus-new-normal/?fbclid=IwAR2qpfnDR7yLg8nF0MeirP1sPltqoK2NLQL-AQhSyKO8eolLGcNgArtj5S0

[6] Peter Brown, *Through the Eye of the Needle: Wealth, the Fall Rome, and the Making of Christianity in the West, 350-550 AD (Princeton and Oxford: Princeton University Press, 2012).*

[7] Deenabandhu Manchala, From afar, yet together in struggle and hope," (10 June 2020). https://www.globalministries.org/from_afar_yet_together_in_struggle_and_hope? fbclid=IwAR1_lFPYWrQCaHdc6evlyGD7nBUk3dBL k7HEWt3RkkYAAQXr3YMQm1xuUNk

[8] Walter Brueggemann, "Is there Anything Impossible for God?" (11 June 2020). https://churchanew.org/blog/2020/06/11/brueggemann5?fbclid=IwAR1LLNhSBO6mN5sNse5ZArfrjxVbSM1lcgOExE PSp0GBE91RivoXUPBbKm0

[9] Rebecca Solnit, "'The impossible has already happened': what coronavirus can teach us about hope," (7 April 2020). https://www.theguardian.com/world/2020/apr/07/what-coronavirus-can-teach-us-about-hope-rebecca-solnit

[10] Joerg Rieger, "The Ugly truth of a Pandemic and the Logic of Downturn," (9 April 2020). https://religionandjustice.squarespace.com/blog/the-ugly-truth-of-a-pandemic-and-the-logic-of-downturn

[11] https://sojo.net/articles/kairos-moment?fbclid=IwAR1Fap7qRNjJ33Gr WWysHgQUCEXnMjCcA-dXMZ1sXeOEWi2eS5ibqBYgi6A

12 Brueggemann, *Virus as a Summons to* Faith, Kindle Edition, 32.

13 Mary Pezzulo, "George Floyd and the American Apocalypse," (5 June 2020). https://www.patheos.com/blogs/steelmagnificat/2020/06/george-floyd-and-the-american-apocalypse/

14 Catherine Keller, "A Letter from Catherine Keller," (2 April 2020). https://medium.com/@dostlund_42808/a-letter-from-catherine-keller-1930029c4914

15 Keller, "A Letter from Catherine Keller."

A Liturgy for COVID Times[1]

INTERROGATION: *Let us ask God*

(Set to the tune of *Were you there when they crucified my Lord?*)[2]

1. Were You there when they found it hard to breathe?

    Were You there when they found it hard to breathe?

    Oh, sometimes it causes me to tremble, tremble, tremble.

    Were You there when they found it hard to breathe?
    (Silence)

2. Were You there when we knelt and prayed for them?

    Were You there when we knelt and prayed for them?

    Oh, sometimes it causes me to tremble, tremble, tremble.

    Were You there when we knelt and prayed for them?
    (Silence)

3. Were You there when our faith nor work saved them?

    Were You there when our faith nor work saved them?

    Oh, sometimes it causes me to tremble, tremble, tremble.

    Were You there when our faith nor work saved them?
    (Silence)

4.   Were You there when they left this world alone?

Were You there when they left this world alone?

Oh, sometimes it causes me to tremble, tremble, tremble.

Were You there when they left this world alone?
(Silence)

5.   Were You there when they're thrown to fire and grave?

Were You there when they're thrown to fire and grave?

Oh, sometimes it causes me to tremble, tremble, tremble.

Were You there when they're thrown to fire and grave?
(Silence)

6.   Were You there when their loved ones grieved and wept?

Were You there when their loved ones grieved and wept?

Oh, sometimes it causes me to tremble, tremble, tremble.

Were You there when their loved ones grieved and wept?
(Silence)

INTERRUPTION: *Let God speak*

Not in the great wind,
We hear the still small voice of God

Not in the earthquake,
We hear the still small voice of God

Not in the fire,
We hear the still small voice of God

But in sheer silence,
We hear the still small voice of God

Reviving our spirits

We hear the still small voice of God

Assuring us solace

We hear the still small voice of God

(Silence)

INVITATION: *Let God restore us*

Although COVID limits our chances of celebrating Eucharist as a sacrament within a sanctuary, it cannot stop us from enjoying Eucharist as a communion present at all times and at all places. When we are distressed and anguished, the Lord invites us to this restoring fellowship.

Under the solitary broom tree, I sit and pray,

"It is enough; now, O Lord, take away my life."

 "Get up and eat."

Alone, we suffer.

"Come to me, I will give you rest."

At the shore of Galilee, besides the charcoal fire,

With fish on it, and bread, He invites,

"Come and have breakfast."

Confused, we wait.

"Come to me, I will give you rest."

At Emmaus, He sat down at table, blessed the bread and broke it,

And gave it to us, saying,

Take. Eat.

Shaken, we grieve.

"Come to me, I will give you rest."

As we remain seated or standing, let us sing the third stanza of the hymn, *What a friend we have in Jesus*:

Are we weak and heavy laden,
Cumbered with a load of care?
Precious Saviour, still our refuge--
Take it to the Lord in prayer!
Do your friends despise, forsake you?
Take it to the Lord in prayer!
In His arms He'll take and shield you;
You will find a solace there.

INTROSPECTION: *Let us examine ourselves*
In such a time as this,
We often failed to be brave
In such a time as this,
We often failed to serve
In such a time as this,
We often failed to love

In such a time as this,
We often failed to care
In such a time as this,
We often failed to share
In such a time as this,
We often failed to cheer

In such a time as this,
We often failed to trust
In such a time as this,
We often failed to rest

In such a time as this,
We often failed to be just

Forgive us, O Lord
Heal us and renew us.

(*Prayer in Silence*)

Your faith has healed you. Go in peace,
Amen! Thanks be to God.

INSTRUCTION: *Let us listen to the Word of God*

Let us all joining in singing the hymn *Love to Live* (set to the tune of *Love Divine, All Loves Excelling)*[3]. As we sing this Hymn, let us prepare ourselves to listen to the Word of God.

Broken, shattered, left ov'rpowered
Seeing humanity decline
Pain and grief were thrust upon us
Joy vanished to be no more
Death gave life to fear, anxiety
Wondered if our time had come
Clung to hope like child grasps mother
While each day we drudged along.

Sick, poor, migrants, aged, and homeless
Faced the brunt of brutal loss
Did God cause it? Can God stop it?
Our minds probed with fleeting doubt
Where was God in all this suffering?
Had God's mighty right hand failed?
Through each passing love persisted
Life survived against all odds

Streets abandoned; doors not opened
Hearts were parched as gatherings ceased
Faith being tested turned to action
Care, compassion knew no bounds
Church no longer was confined by
Boundaries, altars, and priesthood
Church as event sprung all over
Paving way for love to live

HOMILY

INSPIRATION: *Let us proclaim our inspired faith*

Who will separate us from the love of Christ? /

Will hardship, /or distress, /or persecution, /or famine, / or nakedness, /or peril, /or sword?

No, /in all these things /we are more than conquerors / through Him who loved us.

For I am convinced that /neither death, /nor life, /nor angels, /nor rulers, /nor things present, /nor things to come, /nor powers, /nor height, /nor depth, /nor anything else in all creation, /will be able to separate us /from the love of God /in Christ Jesus our Lord.

(Romans 8: 35, 37 – 39)

INTERCESSION: *Let us intercede*
(Based on Pope Francis' reflection on St Mark 4:35-41 – Jesus calming the storm)

It is evening,
Thick darkness has gathered over our squares, our streets, and our cities

The deafening silence and a distressing void,
We feel everywhere. We find ourselves afraid and lost.

Gale blowing, waves breaking, boat swamped,
It is pain, anxiety and uncertainty.
The refugees, the migrants, and vulnerable are we,
"Lord, do you not care that we are perishing?"

We are in the same boat,
Irrespective of class, caste, race, age, gender, religion and language,
Fragile and disoriented, afraid and lost,
We row together. We need each other. We pray together.

In Unison

God,
A time of -
Pain and anguish,
Suffering and distress,
Fear and confusion;
May we be protected under the shadow of Your mercy.

Broken and shattered -
You accompany us.
Concerned and confused –
You counsel us.
Distanced and quarantined –
You embrace us.
Rejected and abandoned –
You empower us.
Ailing and dying –
You heal us.

Believing that,
Even death cannot separate us from Your love,
Together may we rejoice in Your peace,
In Christ Jesus our Lord, Amen.

In silence, let us remember all those who are infected and affected by COVID.

Let us sum up all our petitions, using the words of Lord's Prayer, praying boldly,

Our Father/Mother/Parent, hallowed be Your name, Your kingdom come, Your will be done, on earth as in heaven. Give us today our daily bread. Forgive us our sins as we forgive those who sin against us. Lead us not into temptation but deliver us from evil. For the kingdom, the power, and the glory are yours now and forever. Amen.

Let us listen to His voice –
Peace! Be still. Peace! Be still.

Let us share His peace –
Peace be with you. Peace be with you.

The Church as event, amidst COVID, is called to become the harbinger of hope and peace. Therefore, let us join together in singing, as we commit ourselves to a daily living to pray together, care each other and strive towards a promising future.

Hymn (Set to the tune of *The Church's One Foundation*)[4]

The Church as Event is a living Church of God
The Church is where we gather to worship God of love
The Son has sacrificed life and offered life for all
The Spirit leads and heals us, from death, disease and dearth

The Church will manifest the full glory of our God
In bodies of all people, with hearts and minds in love
The Church will direct us to new life and life to all
Renewing every mind, and sustaining every breath.

Though we are broken-hearted, children of our God
Protect, respect and honour the life we share in love.
We come around the table with gifts, songs, prayers for all
We come to mend the broken, choosing life over death.

The calling is to be oriented by our God
Our streets are full of life and protesting out of love
The Church should care for all earth and none is spared at all
Let's strive for justice, freedom, equality and health.

INTERMISSION: *Let us pause and prepare*
Church remains. Worship continues.
Life moves. Love compels.
Grace fills us. Spirit strengthens.
Cross invites. Crown awaits.

Hence, we pause – an intermission,
To bless each other

The Lord be with you
And also with you.
Let us depart in peace.
In the name of the Lord. Amen

Praise God, from whom all blessings flow;
Praise Him, all creatures here below;
Praise Him above, ye heav'nly host;
Praise Father, Son, and Holy Ghost! Amen

Endnotes

[1] This liturgy is prepared by Viji Varghese Eapen, an ordained minister in the Church of South India, currently pursuing his PhD in Dublin City University, Ireland.

[2] Lyrics by Viji Varghese Eapen

[3] Lyrics by Arvind Theodore, PhD student, Union Theological Seminary, New York.

[4] Concept: Dr. Cláudio Carvalhaes / Lyrics: Moses Shanthi Kumar Bollam John, PhD student, Union Theological Seminary, New York.

Afterword

*Revelation E. Velunta**

"We are on the same boat."
"We are all in this together."
"We will get through this together."

These statements have been repeated so many times on TV, in radio, in print, and on social media in the past eight months that there are those who have begun to believe they are true. Mothy Varkey in his *Church and Diakonia in the Age of COVID-19* disagrees.

If I can summarise the work that Mothy Varkey has offered in this book, it is about exposing the untruths behind the "we are on the same boat" propaganda of the privileged, the powerful, and the propertied. And he does this by using ekklesia and diakonia as hermeneutical lenses.

Varkey reclaims, deconstructs and decolonises ekklesia and diakonia. Ekklesia, which has been translated as church, has never been and will never be a building. It has always been gathered assemblies or called-out communities or congregations. Plural. The expression of this ekklesia is diakonia. Diakonia, for Varkey, is more than service. It is being immersed in people's struggles for freedom, sanctity of life, peace based on justice, and integrity of creation. Ekklesia in its diakonia takes sides by creating subversive faith communities.

From the caste system to ecology, from economics to poverty, from Apple and Google to bicycles and Cuba, Varkey's ekklesial and diakonial lenses expose the imperial and capitalist underpinnings of the "we are in the same boat" propaganda. His lenses also bring to the fore peoples and movements and their alternative economies of life.

If "we" means everyone then, as this book has discussed, we definitely are not on the same boat during this raging storm called COVID-19. A select few are in five-star cruise ships. And their wealth has quadrupled during this pandemic! Many are packed like sardines in smaller boats. Many more are holding on to anything and everything that floats, their heads barely out of the water. The majority are in the raging waters, struggling to survive, crying out for help.

But there are those, reminding us who call ourselves Christian, who do what Peter did when there was a raging storm in the Sea of Galilee. They get out of their boats because Jesus is not in the boat. He is in the waters.

Calling then and calling us now. To follow.

* **Dr. Revelation E. Velunta** is Associate Professor of New Testament and Cultural Studies at Union Theological Seminary, Philippines.